I read Michelle Smith's book in one sitting and was incredibly touched! I believe she will give hope to many women who may feel that life has been unfair. Michelle, by her willingness to be vulnerable and honest, has been a catalyst to showcase the enormity of God's grace and redemption.

My prayer is that this book will get into the hands of those who have been victimized by the enemy. I know Michelle's testimony will continue to be a great blessing!

—Cathy Lechner
Speaker, Author
Covenant Ministries

A heart-tugging story expressed through personal letters of gratitude, describing pain of the past and moving to healing, forgiveness and hope in Christ.

—Esther Burroughs
Speaker, Author
Treasures of the Heart Ministry

I can't remember when I've read a more poignant and emotionally gripping testimony of God's enduring and unending grace.

—Barbara Curnutt
Executive Director
Georgia WMU and Women's Ministry

To: [redacted]

you
are so pretty!
your true
beauty
shines from
within!

Michelle
Smith

Ps 37:4

READY TO WALK

Michelle Smith

CREATION HOUSE PRESS

Ready to Walk by Michelle Smith
Published by Creation House Press
A part of Strang Communications Company
600 Rinehart Road
Lake Mary, FL 32746
www.charismahouse.com

Library of Congress Card Number: 00-111322
International Standard Book Number: 0-88419-761-1

To inquire about availability for
speaking engagements,
please contact: Michelle Smith
P.O. Box 10023
Pensacola, FL 32524-0023

01 02 03 04 05 8 7 6 5 4 3 2 1
Printed in the United States of America

DEDICATION

To my Lord and Savior,
Jesus Christ:
I have poured out my life
on these pages; may it be an acceptable
drink offering to by used for Your glory alone.
Thank You, Jesus, for my life.

ACKNOWLEDGMENTS

Writing my book has been a true journey. I praise my Jesus for giving me a host of encouragers along the path:

First of all, my husband, Rob, who has been a constant and consistent voice of affirmation.

My children, Lindsey and Bobby, who have inspired me as I have watched their gifts flourish, free from the chains of generations past.

Reverend Henry Roberts, a pastor, author and friend who was sensitive and obedient to the still small voice of the Holy Spirit. He called me one day not knowing why. Only God knew I had prayed about speaking to him to seek advice on how to begin writing a book. I will forever be grateful and cherish the times I received his wise counsel.

Pat Brinson, my personal editor, who sifted through and ordered my thoughts and words. She remained sensitive to me and to the Holy Spirit.

My dear friend, Joyce Lewis, who typed for me in the beginning and encouraged me to the end.

Suzanne Riddle, my official typist, whose patience and kindness have been very soothing.

Margaret Jackson, who modeled for me Christian forgiveness. It was her influence that began to soften the words on the pages of my book.

Melody Weber, who was the spiritual catalyst for connecting this book to Creation House Press.

Creation House Press, who offered this glorious opportunity. Thank you!

May God alone be glorified!
Amen

Contents

To My Reader:

The book you are about to read is my testimony. Written over a four-year period, it covers forty-five years of one life blessed by God. Each chapter is a letter I have written to a person who has been used by God to touch me with His love. Since the letters are arranged in the order I wrote them, you will recognize a hardness of heart that gradually softens as you turn the pages. For me to write this book, my loving heavenly Father allowed my heart to break as I remembered my youth. You will hear my heart cry out as its broken pieces are pounded into fine dust. As my story continues, you will see the Lord begin to sift out the unneeded debris of anger, bitterness and shame.

I feel the Lord has kept the promise He made in Ezekiel 36:26–27:

> I will give you a new heart and put a new spirit in you; I will remove from you your heart of stone and give you a heart of flesh. And I will put my Spirit in you and move you to follow my decrees and be careful to keep my laws.

Like the potter with clay, God has molded me a new heart. I see now that He was mixing the crushed particles of my broken spirit with His clear, clean, living water.

Writing this book has been a cleansing experience. I was tempted to go back and clean up and soften each letter; however, I believe the Lord has led me to leave them as they were written. Recognizing the process and the progress is to bring glory to the ultimate Potter. I thank Him for the closeness and intimacy of His hands as He was remolding my heart. My prayer is that my book will be used as a vessel for Him, a vessel of hope.

I desperately hope this book will deliver an encouraging word to you. The pain I have suffered is not the worst imaginable, but it is my pain. I am willing to share it with others so they can see that our God truly does work all things together for good. (See Romans 8:28.) As I reflect back on my life, I see that Jesus was there all along. I can see His light and feel His touch through each of the saints I address. None of them had any idea he or she was being used in such a powerful way. It is the little acts of kindness that make a difference. I have learned to give because of those who have given to me.

Thank you, my reader, for picking up this book. I pray for you that, as you share my journey, the eyes of your heart will be enlightened. May you recognize your Savior on the faces of those who have offered you a drink of living water on your own journey. May your own life be a drink offering to others in the name of Jesus.

To God be the glory!

—MICHELLE SMITH
JANUARY 25, 1999

I

HELEN

Dear Helen,

They tell me that you were there when I came home from the hospital, a newborn. My memories of you are of warmth—warm eyes, warm smile, warm heart. You were round and soft to hug. Your hands smelled like Clorox. I wondered if all the cleaning had bleached your palms white!

To my mother you were the colored cleaning woman. To me you were an angel in disguise. For $10 one day a week for seven years, you made a priceless difference in my life.

Did you know how it was in our house? Did you know that, no matter how well you cleaned, when you closed the door behind you, our home felt dirty again?

You knew, of course, that my father was a car salesman. It was a good living for someone who had only eight years of schooling. He was proud that he (and the bank) owned our red brick rowhouse in Baltimore. He paid his bills, gave my mother enough to run the house and therefore was entitled to do anything he pleased. I can remember an occasional Saturday or Sunday evening when he was home, but on week-nights, he rewarded himself with trips to local bars with his friends.

It was a routine that infuriated my mother. She was able to maintain control in every area of her life except my father's drinking. This was not due to lack of trying, for she approached every task with the determination of a tiger. She went after locating which bar my father had chosen like a wild animal searching for prey. We had an address/phone book with every bar in Baltimore. She began calling at dinnertime and didn't give up until she found him. From her side, the conversation was all screaming. My father either blew her off or got so angry that he came home to continue screaming it out. After a while, he began to have the bartenders lie for him and say he wasn't there. At that news, she would pace the floor like a caged animal, sometimes for hours.

At night I sought refuge under my bed covers, trying to block out the fear with sleep. Many nights, however, I was forced out of my dreams and into a nightmare. My mother frantically pulled back the covers and shook me out of bed. Sometimes she dressed me, roughly pulling off my pajamas and jerking on my clothes. Sometimes she told me to get dressed by myself, but it seemed I could never do it fast enough to please her. I quickly learned not to cry or whine. My mother hated both of those reactions and responded with wild rounds of slapping and screaming. On nights when she felt especially desperate, I never changed out of my pajamas. It didn't matter. My mother was on a mission. We were to drive past every bar until we spotted Daddy's car.

As I write this, I can vividly remember the scene from the movie *101 Dalmatians* when the cruel villainess vehemently drove off in wild pursuit of the Dalmatian puppies. The look in her eyes was the same look that possessed my mother.

My eyes showed only terror. She drove like a madwoman. She reluctantly obeyed red lights and stop signs. An obstacle in the way was cursed and damned. Green lights were permission to slam on the gas pedal and proceed with full speed. She swerved corners and jumped curbs. It was like being on a roller coaster with the devil. When we finally spotted his car, my mother would pull into the parking lot with the determination of a vulture. I was left in the car while she went to retrieve the fallen prey.

There were times when he still had a lot of life left in him. He was livid and ready to fight. Usually, she managed to convince him not to drive, but I cowered as they shouted all the way home. Other times he was like a big, ugly rag doll with a blown-up red face that drooled and stared out with blank glassy eyes. On those nights, we stuffed him into the back seat and listened to him mumble all the way home. The smell of stale beer and smoke permeated our car.

Once we got home, we had the challenge of getting my father in the house quietly and without his falling. If there were an alcoholic olympics for this feat, he would have gotten a bronze medal, owing it all to his coach, my mother. However, she never stopped trying for the gold, achieveable only by hiding all evidence of the night's activities from our neighbors. He usually lost points for shouting or moaning when he tripped over his unsteady feet and hit the ground.

In the morning, he was the one she shook from the bed. I would wake up to the same sound each time. When I got older, I remember thinking she ought to record her routine and play it back because it was always the same. He rarely said a word. Sometimes I felt sorry for him. However, he was smart. He allowed her to think she had some control as she ranted on and on. He knew she would wear out and cool down eventually. He also knew he had no intention of allowing anything to prevent him from drinking whenever he pleased. Her wrath was merely an unpleasant side-effect.

There was one tactic she tried during those morning tirades that involved me as the pawn. I hated it. She called me in, made me tell Daddy how bad he was the night before, and then forced him to put his hand on my head and swear on my life that he would never drink again. I lived in fear of death every time he drank.

I wished I could die rather than tell my daddy he was bad. He was my daddy, and I loved him. He read "The Night Before Christmas" to me every Christmas Eve and tried to appear like Santa in my eyes year round. Quite often he came bearing gifts for me after one of his drunken sleigh rides. My mother usually returned them or put them away.

At that time she appeared to be the wicked witch who caused him to run to a bottle for escape, but I know now that he was really trying to escape the demons that were buried deep within. Drinking merely provided him with a mask of numbness.

My mother had her own means of numbing her pain. In a desperate attempt to survive living at the mercy of my father's alcoholism, my mother found solace in her own addiction, a liquid green tranquilizer called Butisol. Working for doctors on and off all her life gave my mother a self-conferred medical degree. She certainly knew how to talk the talk and proceeded to order herself drugs whenever she deemed it necessary. Between drug reps and a family friend who owned a small pharmacy, we were well-stocked. We had drugs for every ailment imaginable. One thing's for sure: She never ran out of the green medicine.

The green medicine made my mother a monster. Her tolerance was minimal, and there were no boundaries to shield her from the burning inner rage. There were times that rage was directed at my father. Other times, it was directed at me. As I think about my childhood, many of my memories revolve around finding a safe place to hide. All the large pieces of mahogany furniture in the dining room served as a fortress protecting me from a crazy woman, but nothing could protect me from the inner voices that told me I was a bad little girl and my badness was the reason I had such a mean mommy.

One night, I saw a big ray of light circling the sky—probably one of those advertising spotlights. When I asked my mother what it was, she told me that it was a light looking for bad little girls. I hid behind the liquor cabinet in the living room for hours. When my mother found me and learned why I was there, she laughed at me. Her mocking made me feel worse. I was convinced that my mommy was so mean because I was such a bad girl.

I wonder, Helen, if you remember me as a crying, whiny little girl. I cried a lot—about everything. I still cry too much, and I hate it. My mother seemed to hate it also. Any sign of weakness seemed to cause her to strike out.

The scariest place in the house was the kitchen, where my mother spent most of her time. She said it made her feel secure. An Italian, she had a pot of spaghetti sauce on the stove almost all the time. To this day, there are times when I have to fight those feelings of nausea that consume me when I smell red sauce.

Being called into the kitchen always scared me. There were so many possible weapons and nowhere to hide. It was so small that I felt trapped. If I cried or whined or even sniffed, she would lash out. Whatever was in her hand went flying. Red sauce splattered like drops of blood. On the inside of one of the cabinets was a metal rack with black-handled metal utensils. When that door swung open and she reached for one of those dreaded utensils, I dove under the table for protection. All I did was trap myself. She would pull me out and beat me. It seemed her goal was to cover every part of my body. She struck up and down both legs and then began on my arms. There were always a few blows on my back. The worst part was the end, when she released the remains of her rage on my head.

Helen, this is so hard to write about, even after thirty-five years. I wonder if you knew. If you did, you never judged us. You believed I was a good, sweet little girl, and I felt good when you were there. Do you see why I cherished your presence in our home? Your presence granted a reprieve because Mother did not beat me when you were there. She sometimes even showed me tenderness. No one could be bad when you were with us because the goodness of the Lord was shining through you. You were a light in our dark, dark world.

As I look back, I can see you formed my early opinions of black people. I thought every black person was like you. Maybe that is why my life has been blessed with many positive relationships with other black people. Prejudice in reverse. I expected goodness and kindness, and I have almost always had it returned.

As I launch this effort to write to people who have been most significant in my life, I have to begin with you. I look forward to the day when I can meet you again in heaven so I can thank you for the part you played in God's plan for my life.

II

Karen

My dear Karen,

If I had one wish for every little girl in the world, it would be to have a best friend. It is amazing how close I feel to you after so many years. I often wonder what you look like now. When we were children, you were slender and graceful. Watching you, I felt as if I had opened a jewelry box—you know, the kind that had a tiny doll turning to a gentle tune. Actually, your house, up the street from ours, was my special box. It wasn't a perfect household, of course, but love's tune could be heard there. I needed to hear it more than I could ever express in the words of a child. Now that I am an adult, I'd like to tell you why you were so important to me.

You often told me my mother was mean. She *was* mean, and I loved to hear you say it. Of course, you told me your mother was mean, too, and I probably agreed with you at the time. I know now that your mother was not mean; she was a mother. I remember the time she spanked you with a ruler because you had a sassy mouth. You were greatly insulted that she spanked you with your own ruler. I couldn't believe that was all there was to your spanking. My spankings were much worse. In fact, they weren't spankings at all. They were beatings that left bruises all over my legs and arms. My mother said the bruises were my "bad marks"; if I told others how I got them, they would know how bad I had been. If your mother noticed, my mother would tell her I had fallen down the steps. Because I was clumsy and I did fall a lot, it was easy to believe.

My mother wanted the neighbors to believe she had control over every aspect of her life, including her child. This was the only way she could continue to save face, knowing that there was one area over which she had no control: my father's drinking.

As I write, I will imagine we are in your room, hiding as your sister, Carol Ann, searches for her Sissy and a welcome playmate. We huddle in the back of your closet, pushing all of your and Carol Ann's shoes away with our feet. With the sashes of all your full-skirted dresses hanging down and tickling our foreheads, we would talk softly so Carol Ann would not find us. I did a lot of talking, but the "secrets" I shared had little to do with the dark secrets in my family. I still see you looking at me with those big blue eyes, listening to every word I say. You always were a great listener. Listen now, my dear Sissy. I want to tell you so I can let this go.

From the day my mother first saw me, she began trying to "fix" me. She told me that when I was born, my head was misshapen. As with many babies, the birth process compressed the soft bones at the top of my skull. She said she worked at correcting this with a warm washcloth, reshaping my head every day until she got it right. How lucky I was supposed to feel that she rounded out my head. I could still be bearing the burden of having a "pelvis head."

She had always wanted me to look just right, but her idea and my idea of just right were never the same. I yearned to have long hair like you and to pull it back into a ponytail, but she told me it was too thick. She had a beauty shop in our basement, remember? The thinning scissors she used on my hair looked like a silver alligator with teeth. Every night, she set my hair in pin curls with metal clips that pressed like little nails against my head when I slept. In the morning, she yanked those out, yelling at me if I had lost any in the night, and tried to fashion my hair in a way that would please her. Once she had achieved her goal, she plastered it with hair spray.

One day, the hair spray smelled different. I opened my eyes and saw in the mirror that she was using Pledge furniture polish. I tried to tell her, but she kept hitting me with a thick plastic comb for talking back. When she finally realized her mistake, my arms were covered with thin red lines from the slaps with the comb. She laughed. I remember frantically searching for my white sweater to cover the "bad marks." It was a hot day, but I never took it off. Later I heard her tell your mother about the Pledge, laughing during the entire tale. This is hard for me to write because I still don't think it's funny. My arms still twinge as I remember. If I had been able to tell you when we were children, you would have rubbed my arms. You were kind and tender to me. I bet you are a good mother.

I struggle with being a good mother. I was afraid to discipline my own little girl because I feared I would become like my mother. I feared I would hit my child and never stop. I couldn't bear to be the mean mommy. I fought my husband's attempts at discipline, seeing them as cruel and harsh, although he was raised in a fairly well-balanced home and has common sense in addition to education. As a result, my little daughter did not learn early boundaries or respect for authority. This failure was painfully made clear when she started school. It was hard for me to accept that my child was not perfect.

I thought it was just me, but I have found many mothers suffer from this feeling. We try hard, and when our children mess up, we feel it is a reflection on us. I did try hard. I have a B.A. degree in education and an M.A. degree in counseling. The two degrees provided me with many skillful ways to over-communicate and almost ruin my child. I was able to distract every undesirable behavior with an alternative activity, encourage desirable behavior with charts and validate every feeling she had. If she and I could have lived in our own little world for the rest of our lives, maybe it would have worked. She still resents that I had a son who came along and forced her to learn to share. There is a whole world out there of unique personalities, and somehow we have to teach our children how to get along with them minus the charts and stars.

Blaming my own mother for not providing me with an appropriate role model was not going to help me raise my daughter. I needed to get past the blame game before I gave her any more reasons for playing it herself in years to come. I tried taking her to a counselor, but the counselor explained that the best way to help her was to help me. She needed someone who cared enough to discipline her. This was especially difficult since I was disciplined so harshly and my real motivation for good behavior had been fear. I was always impressed that you never seemed afraid of your parents.

I married a man who is very much like your father. He is a tall, handsome man with character and high moral standards. My father had the tall and handsome part, plus he had wit and charm. Do you remember how we ran into his arms and he picked us up and swung us around? He was also a generous man. When he took me to the zoo one day, we brought home giant lollipops for you, Carol Ann and me. I remember they had faces made of bubble gum balls. Because your mother was taking care of one of your cousins at the time, she cracked the lollipops into pieces to make fair shares. I thought it was a tragedy. My father felt bad because he hadn't bought four lollipops.

He was never abusive to me, and yet I feared him as much as my mother. I saw him beat my older brother, Dickie, until he bled. Dickie was always in trouble. My father said he was a "bad boy." He would take off his belt and lash out at this skinny teenage boy like a person taming wild animals. I would scream and be pushed upstairs, where I would cry until it was over. Later, I would crawl into Dickie's bed to comfort him.

Dickie was bright but had a hard time in school. I think he was cheated early on of the security of love every child deserves. He had emotional problems stemming back to rejection by his mother, our father's first wife. Being a child herself and unable to cope with a newborn and a husband gone to war, she found comfort outside the bonds of marriage. Facing my father's wrath on his return from the war, she was reluctantly forced to allow her mother to raise her son. My father's weekend visits with gifts and trips for ice cream did not provide Dickie with the parental love he needed. By the time he came to live with our family at age ten, he had developed deviant means to fill the voids in his life. I was made to believe he was a cheat, a liar and a thief. I can see now that he was a desperate little boy, taking whatever he could to fill the holes in his heart. My father could only view his misdeeds as a poor reflection of himself and did his best to beat it out.

My father may have looked like a strong man, but he was weak. He beat our dogs mercilessly. However, he never really gained the control he wanted. Remember that big brown poodle named Cocoa? No matter how often he beat her, no matter how victorious he felt, she never stopped chewing things when she was left alone. Rejection causes one to act out. The dog acted out, my brother acted out, and my father ultimately acted out the most. He lived his life like a scared little boy, hiding with a belt in one hand and a beer in the other.

I don't think I ever saw your father drink. I remember him bringing ice cream home from a restaurant. One of my favorite memories is of your father making omelets for us one morning after I spent the night with you. I had never heard of anyone putting anything inside an omelet until you asked me if I wanted jelly or cheese. I felt so special that he made a jelly omelet just for me.

I pray you have married a man as wonderful as your father. I also pray that you are making the difference in other children's lives that your mother made in mine. I pray that you and Carol Ann are close and that she has forgiven both of us for leaving her out so much. She was always kind to me, and I was undeserving.

Most of all, my dear sweet Sissy, please know that you will forever hold a special place in my heart. Being with you gave my life hope and something to look forward to each day. Thank you for being there.

III

Mrs. Schuchardt

Dear Mrs. Schuchardt,

As I begin to write this, I recall exactly what you looked like when I was in your first-grade class thirty-six years ago. You were my first exposure to formal education. Only rich kids went to kindergarten in those days. Preschool wasn't an option. Yet, I don't believe I could have had a better start. You provided the perfect balance of calmness, compassion and common sense that I so desperately needed.

It was in your class that I was able to hear some positive messages. Although I have lived much of my life haunted by echoes of a sad childhood, I am grateful for the tune of hope the Lord was singing quietly all along. I thank Him that you knew the words to His song and sang them to me that year.

As I write this, I can remember the smell of my new book bag. It was red with black buckles. I longed for a lunch box with a thermos, but my mother considered that extravagant. I carried my lunch in a brown paper bag, and I was instructed to fold it and bring it home every afternoon. Every Monday, I got a new bag. I was afraid that something might happen to my bag. You see, Mrs. Schuchardt, I was afraid of my mother. I could never predict how she would be when I went home. The trick was to figure out ahead of time exactly how displeased she was and how to prevent becoming the target of her displeasure. Life in our home was like being on a battlefield littered with land mines. I had to learn to read looks, gestures and even footsteps to survive. At school, it was a great relief that the only thing I had to read was how Dick and Jane could throw the big red ball to Spot.

Yet, even the big red ball was an issue for me. My mother was prone to throwing things when she was angry, and my automatic response was to duck if anything came my way. Someone told my mother I was ducking the ball during our playground time. I can still hear her laughing as she repeated the story to friends. It never occurred to me then that she was covering up her own guilt. It was only one more reason for me to believe I was worthless.

I can vividly remember the word card and the picture you had for "Mother." When you weren't using it in our reading group, it was placed in a pocket on a manila chart. I remember staring at the picture of "Mother" and thinking how different she was from my own mother. I thought I was a bad little girl because I didn't have a mother like that. Of course, back then our televisions portrayed mothers like June Cleaver or Donna Reed. It took me many years to realize that even good children don't grow up like Timmy with his dog, Lassie. Contrary to popular belief, no one has a perfect home, and only our heavenly Father knows best.

In His great mercy, I became ill that year. Now, having taught first grade and raised two children, I realize that the first school year is a vulnerable time for small bodies. It seems as if the days of runny noses, earaches and sore throats will never end. Back then, tonsils were extracted routinely. Mine were to be taken out during Christmas vacation.

Our family doctor ran some preliminary blood tests and was concerned with the results. Although I never knew the technicalities, my blood count was way off. He filled out a card and told my mother to take me to get more tests. When my mother read the doctor's words "Leukemia suspected," she was so upset she had to get a neighbor to drive us to the hospital.

During the several days required for the tests to be completed, home was the closest to heaven it had ever been. My mother cried every time she put up a Christmas angel. She said that next year she would have her own angel in heaven. I didn't understand anything about blood counts or leukemia. All I knew was that I had a great thing going. My mother was the nicest she had ever been.

I did not have leukemia; however, I had to recover from the blood deficiency before I was admitted to the hospital for the tonsillectomy. I finally went in that February. Except for one shot, every memory of my hospital experience was positive. In fact, I loved it. I was in a place where I was the center of attention. My welfare was first and foremost on everyone's mind. This was a welcome contrast to the main concern that usually consumed us: keeping my father's drinking a secret. For that blessed time, drinking was not as important as I was.

It was a long time before I understood why my daddy was crying when I woke up from my operation. I didn't know that I had hemorrhaged greatly and almost didn't wake up. All I knew was that his eyes were filled with tears of love and not glazed with alcohol.

My recovery time at home was sweet. Along with a comforter made by my great-grandmother, my mother kept me covered with her love and concern.

You came to see me after I came home and brought me valentines from the class. You also brought me a big heart-shaped lollipop. I have wanted to make the children I have taught feel special the same way you made me feel that day. I believe you were the one who showed me how.

My coming back to school after my illness was a challenge for you. I had learned a way to manipulate.

Almost every day, I told you I didn't feel good, and I was sent home sick. Going home sick assured me that my mother would be nice and I would receive good care. I was able to pull those strings for several months. It was easy because I was thin and pale. I had also watched many Shirley Temple movies.

I can still remember the day you looked at me and said, "I am beginning to think that you say you don't feel good just so you can go home." Your tone was gentle but firm. I forget what I said or did, but I remember how I felt. I thought you were the smartest person in the world, and I knew you were right.

Unfortunately, the whole experience set the stage for years of hypochondria. By the grace of God, I am not sick anymore. I no longer hide behind "I don't feel good." I do feel good. Searching my past for answers helped me to see that Jesus has been with me all along. Through people like you, He was taking all the torn pieces and weaving them together for good.

At an impressionable time in my life, you planted seeds that allowed me to bloom and grow in a garden variety of classroom settings and helped shape me into the teacher I always wanted to be. I have been blessed with many opportunities to give back to others the love and care that you gave to me. Thank you, Mrs. Schuchardt. You have touched many lives.

IV

NANA

Dear Nana,

I wonder if you knew the things I am about to tell you. Did you know that when I was a little child, your home was one of the few places of comfort I had?

You made me feel that someone could love me. Little things like having black licorice and cheese curls for me helped me to believe it. You let me choose any rose I desired from your rose bushes. You cut the rose, soaked the stem in a wet napkin, and wrapped it with waxed paper and rubber bands. Even Miss America couldn't have felt more important than I did when you handed me a rose and crowned me with a kiss.

I treasured your hugs, too, Nana. You always smelled like sweet dusting powder. I loved all your dusting powders and perfume bottles. Going into your French Provincial bedroom was like visiting a palace. The first thing I would do is wind up your golden music box. As the music played, I headed straight for the large mirrored tray of perfume bottles on your dresser. I picked up every one every time. I especially remember the dark blue one called "Evening in Paris." After I was satisfied that I had touched every bottle, you let me choose one scent to wear. You taught me to put a tiny bit behind each ear and on my wrists. God was using you, Nana, to spread everywhere the fragrance of the knowledge of Him (See 2 Corinthians 2:15–16.)

One of my favorite pictures of myself as a child is the one of you and me in matching housecoats. I am holding a tiny cake I baked with you. Your kitchen was a happy place for me. I liked the way you let me pick out fresh tea towels for you. You changed them every day. In the same way, God's mercies are new every morning. Yesterday's sins are washed away. In my mother's house the dirty linens were kept on the hook; forgiveness was not allowed. The words "I'm sorry" were worthless. If I told my mother I was sorry, she had a standard reply: "Throw a brick at my head, say you're sorry, and see if the lump goes away." I could never make it better. I was kept on the hook. You and Pop Pop started me on the road that led me to the One who could get me off the hook, to the place where "I'm sorry" is accepted, the only place where we can exchange the dirty towels for the clean ones.

You lived in a row house just like ours. The kitchens were the same size. I hated our kitchen; it made me feel trapped. I loved your kitchen; it made me feel free. At Christmas, you let me sprinkle the red and green sugar on the cookies. At Easter, you let me roll white cream filling into egg shapes before you dipped them in chocolate. You made each holiday a celebration.

My favorite holiday was Thanksgiving. After watching the parade on television in the morning, I couldn't wait to get dressed in my best clothes. I especially liked wearing my black patent leather shoes, hearing them click as I walked as fast as I could from my house to yours. I could feel the warmth the minute I opened the door. The fire in the fireplace was glowing, and the house smelled like turkey. The men were in the basement watching football, and you and my aunts were busy in the kitchen. The table was set in the dining room. I would run to see if the little pilgrim children candles were there. Some years, I made hand-printed place cards to put at each place. Soon the table would be crowded with endless bowls coming from the kitchen. You tried hard to have everyone's favorite vegetable. My special dish was sweet potatoes topped with marshmallows, browned just right. It made me so happy that you made them just for me. My father's favorite dish was creamed broccoli topped with slices of hard-boiled eggs, and my mother's was creamed onions.

It disturbed me that my mother was not kind to you, Nana. I remember thinking if I were you, I wouldn't have made anything just for her. In my young mind, you had every right to treat her like she treated you. Although she blamed you for every poor choice my father made, you treated her like Jesus would have done.

In his blessing, Pop Pop always reminded us that Jesus came to serve us all. Did you ever peek open your eyes to see the rest of us exchanging glances when the prayer went on for a long time? Sometimes they teased Pop Pop about the food getting cold. How I would love to hear him pray again, even the longest of prayers.

Cleaning up after dinner was as much fun as eating. I enjoyed drying each piece of your fine china and placing the silverware into the big wooden box. You praised me and made me feel that I had made a valuable contribution.

In fact, you made a valuable contribution to me. All those rides you arranged for me to the Lutheran Sunday school drove me closer and closer to the saving knowledge that Jesus is real. I can remember the feeling of the Lord's love every time I heard a Bible story. Each Sunday, I brought home a Bible story pamphlet. Although my father refused to go to church, there were many Sunday afternoons he did take time to read me the pamphlet. That is one of my favorite memories of my father. It was the only way the Word of God entered our home. We didn't own a Bible. My mother had been raised to believe that only Catholic priests were holy enough to interpret the Bible.

I am especially grateful for the experience of attending Vacation Bible School. It was like taking all that Sunday school love and multiplying it by five. I cherished everything from the popsicle-stick art projects to the juice and cookie snacks.

I have an early memory of knocking over a small Dixie cup of juice at snack time. I watched in horror as the sticky liquid spread all over the table and onto the napkin holding my two flower-shaped butter cookies. I shuddered in fear, anticipating the consequences. I wanted so badly to run and hide, but I felt a hand touching me gently on the shoulder. A pair of understanding eyes assured me, "It's okay. We can clean it up." I forget the woman's name or even how she looked. I remember her touch and her compassion. It was the touch of God and the compassion of His Son. I look forward to teaching Bible school every summer. My prayer is that I can be used to touch children's lives in the same way mine was touched.

Nana, you planted seeds of faith. You helped me to believe that Someone could love me. The seeds you planted are now growing at the foot of the cross. They bloom and grow like the little flowers you planted along the walkway to your house. Thank you for starting me on my way to Jesus. Because of Him, I know one day I will be able to go again to my grandparents' house, now in heaven. Once again, I will feel the warmth the minute the door is opened, and I will know I am welcomed there.

V

Sister John Francis

Dear Sister John Francis,

When I met you on my seventh birthday, October 3, 1960, it was the first time I had talked to a nun. Your eyes greeted me with such warmth. I felt I had been let in from the cold. I thought you were beautiful, like a statue of a saint. When you found out it was my birthday, you took me to your desk and gave me some treasures: a few holy cards, a rosary and, I think, a holy water holder. I remember feeling as if I had been handed priceless jewels. I can still see your long, slender fingers gently placing them in my small hands.

At seven years old, I could not understand the blanket of sadness that covered our home. I just knew I was under it, and I was not strong enough to lift it off. After my illness the year before had brought me a feeling of being loved and wanted, the world had again turned dark for me.

My brother encountered discipline problems in the Marines and was eventually discharged. He was also discharged from our family. My father disowned him, and I was told never to mention his name again. I was devastated. Not only did I miss my brother, I feared that I, too, could be exiled. My father said he was a "bad boy," and my mother was constantly reminding me that I was a "bad girl."

At school, I had to face a new teacher, who was impossible to please. She seemed to have a heart of stone and a face to match. I felt like a failure.

I was not the only one who felt that way. For my father, who was a patriotic World War II veteran, having a son who left the military under unfavorable conditions was more than he could bear. He numbed his feelings of failure, as always, with alcohol, but his violent outbursts became more frequent and intense. The steel armor my mother wore to convince the neighbors that everything was okay began to show signs of chinks. When at last some of our neighbors were allowed to see the scared, vulnerable woman who hid under the coat of armor, they convinced her to talk to a priest.

My mother had rejected the Catholic Church when she married my father. It was the second marriage for both of them, and she rebelled against her sentence of excommunication. It must have been hard to seek out a priest. But by doing so, at long last she could speak openly and reveal the private hell she tried so hard to disguise. I am grateful that the priest who counseled her cared more about people than rules. The priest convinced her to return to the church, though she would not be allowed to receive communion. (Sister, would Jesus have made such a rule?) She decided I should become Catholic also. I was baptized a Catholic the day I met you.

I cherished every Monday afternoon because that was the day the parish priest picked me up from school and brought me to you. The short time with you was a reprieve from the dark world at home and school that year.

My religious background, up to that point, had been in the Lutheran Church, where my father's parents had taken me. My mother decided not to tell my grandparents of the change to the Catholic Church because she assumed they would protest. When they learned about it, they were hurt because they had not been told. My mother insisted they were angry because my religion had changed. There was an ugly exchange of words, and the family was split. Then the worst possible scenario I could imagine came true. My parents told me I could no longer see my grandparents. It broke my heart, for my grandparents were my greatest source of unconditional love. At age seven, I lost my brother and my grandparents.

On May 17 that year, God changed the circumstances of my life, as only He can do. My mother had been sewing in the basement, working on my First Holy Communion dress. I longed to have one the church was selling, which was fancy with stiff white crinolines and lots of lace. When I ventured to tell my mother, the familiar glare darted at me from behind the sewing machine, and I wished I had never said anything. She was incensed that I would dare want anything other than the white cotton dress she was making. I can remember falling up the stairs, frantically trying to escape her wrath.

Whenever my mother sewed, she used a brown paper lunch bag for clipped threads. Before she went to bed that night, she had emptied an ashtray into the bag, not realizing some of the ashes were still hot. The bag caught fire and destroyed the basement, then fiercely blazed a trail leading upstairs to the kitchen. My mother was awakened by the strangling smoke that invaded the entire second floor.

I remember her shaking me out of bed. I thought I must have done something wrong and was about to be beaten. It was either that, or we were about to go out and search the bars for my father. I think I was actually relieved that the house was on fire. I have always remembered the whole thing as more of an adventure rather than a trauma. I don't remember seeing any flames, just smoke. At the double windows in their bedroom, my mother stood on one side while my father held me out the other. He has permanent lung damage from breathing the smoke in the room while he held me out. We all yelled, "Help! Help!" Every now and then, my father had to bring me in so he could stick out his head and get air. I remember the floor was hot, and he did not let me stand long before he picked me up again. I was his first concern. That night, I felt secure in his hands. I cherish that memory.

No one was coming to help. My parents began to discuss the possibility of jumping into some bushes down below, but I can't remember feeling afraid, just excited. Finally, a neighbor came with a ladder, and I was taken immediately to my best friend's house.

While my parents remained outside watching the flames disappear under the shower of the fire hoses, several neighborhood women tended to me. They put me in the bathtub. The water had to be constantly changed because it kept turning black.

I was allowed to crawl into bed with my best friend. Disappointed that she was asleep, I forced myself to cough until she woke up so that we could talk. Then fear overcame me as I was called back out into the hall. I was afraid I was in trouble for waking her up. The fear increased as I realized my mother was there. I was more afraid of my mother than anything, even a fire.

Miraculously, it seemed that there was a change in my mother. The look in her tear-filled eyes confused me. She hugged me and told me how happy she was that I was alive. She had been afraid that I was dead when she tried to wake me up. Her true fear was that she had been my killer.

Miraculously, two fires were extinguished that night. My mother finally confessed to the priest that she had been beating me to release the rage that burned within her. In an attempt to alleviate her guilt, the priest told my mother that God punished her by having our house catch on fire. What a sad portrayal of our Lord! I believe the fire was His merciful way of destroying a house haunted by demons.

The house was destroyed, but, unfortunately, the demons were not. Our house was remodeled, and eventually, the demons rejoined us. However, my mommy no longer used me as the target for her lack of control. Tragically, she became her own target—but that is another letter.

I finally got my wish, and I had a fancy communion dress just like the other girls. It was lent to me by someone in the parish. The dress my mother made burned away that night, along with the glare in her eyes. I wasn't sure what had happened, but my life regained hope. I made my First Holy Communion on May 20, 1960. I felt like a beautiful little bride. How truly grateful I am that a bride of Christ had been there that year when I needed you so badly to show me the love of Jesus.

I will always love you. Thank you, Sister.

VI

Mrs. McNulty

Dear Mrs. McNulty,

I have often thought of you and recalled a lesson you taught me as my third-grade teacher over thirty years ago. I consider it one of the most valuable lessons I have ever learned.

Third grade represented a beginning for me. The inside of my house had completely burned during the previous spring, but by fall, everything was rebuilt and replaced. Although a house fire would be considered a trauma for most children, I have always remembered it fondly. My neighbors took care of me, my teacher gave me special attention, and my mommy got nicer. If only it had burned away my daddy's desire to drink. Unfortunately, that fire was beyond our control. We continued to live behind a smoke screen of secrets.

However, since the abuse toward me had subsided, I felt I had more control. I just had to be a good girl because I honestly thought that when I was "good," my mother became a "good" mommy. I needed and wanted approval. I desperately tried to please everyone. I am still trying to let go of that need.

I remember that you came in the middle of the second term as the replacement for a young, pretty teacher who was pregnant. Back then, that word wasn't used, and teachers had to stop teaching before their pregnancies began to show.

In contrast to the soft-spoken ways of the previous teacher, you seemed like a drill sergeant because your approach was no-nonsense and direct. At the beginning, I decided I didn't like you. Once I realized your firm approach was fair, however, I began to like you, and I wanted you to like me, too. I could tell you did when you asked me to stay in the room and watch your purse while you took the class to the lavatory.

After watching your purse every day for a week, I decided one day to look inside. I don't remember seeing anything except the gold clip-clasp on your wallet. I opened the clasp and pulled out a quarter. I felt no shame, only excitement, as I planned how to spend it. The next day, I bought a new box of crayons at the school store. I can still recall the smell and the thrill of seeing the eight sharp colored points as I opened the box. There is nothing more rewarding than having a brand-new box of crayons, whole crayons with sharp new points, not broken pieces rounded down from coloring. New crayons make your work neater and, besides, the yellow is still yellow. No little dark spots are on it from coloring next to other colors. Once that happens, yellow is never pure again. Of course, neither was my "good girl" record. I had stolen a quarter, bought crayons and never felt guilty. I still can't believe I did this.

The next time you asked me to watch your purse, I never had to open it. There were three dimes sitting on your desk. I took them and put them in a neat little stack in the corner of my desk; I was already planning my next shopping spree at the school store.

The class came in and sat down. After a few minutes, you told the class that you were disappointed that some money was missing from your desk. You encouraged the person who took it to come forward before lunch period and return the money. I was frozen in fear. I could not imagine how I could go to your desk and confess. I still feel sick as I write.

Lunch period was torture. Everyone was talking about the crime. All the third-grade detectives had theories. Having no idea in the world how to play it cool, I said over and over, "I know everyone thinks it was me, but I didn't do it." Brilliant!

Returning to the classroom after lunch was like marching into a furnace. You came on strong. You said you knew that someone in the class had taken the money, and you would find it. I can clearly remember taking the three dimes from my desk and putting them in the slot made by the sewn-on sash of my dress. You gave us a writing assignment of some sort, but I could not concentrate. Fear and guilt were churning my stomach into knots. I finally asked if I could go to the lavatory.

Once there, I felt a little safer, but I was afraid to go back to the classroom. After a while, you sent someone to check on me. Grasping for straws, I told the other child I had found the missing dimes in the bathroom, and I asked her to take the money to you. I guess I thought I could return to the room, no questions asked. Before I could get myself together and leave the bathroom, you were there.

You calmly told me that finding the dimes in the bathroom just didn't make sense. I was caught. I had no answers. I confessed. After that, I was hysterical. I cried and begged you not to tell my mother. I pleaded and cried. I could not be quieted. I don't remember what you were saying or doing. All I remember is telling you over and over I was sorry and desperately beseeching you not to tell my mother. I was more afraid that day than I have ever been. My mother had not beaten me since the night of the fire, but I had been living in terror that it could happen at any time. I was sure this would be a reason for her to kill me. As I write this, I am aware that my fingers are so tight around my pen that they are aching. My heart is racing, and my stomach is in knots. I feel as if it is happening right now.

But then you looked at me, holding my shoulders, and said, "I am not going to tell your mother." I have never been so relieved. You told me you would not tell anyone. I was to wash my face, and you would explain that I had gotten sick from the greasy fried chicken. You forgave me, took away my penalty and gave me an alibi. I did not get what I deserved. Instead, you gave me what I needed. You gave me grace.

I didn't know Jesus as my Savior back then, but He knew me. He was there. Just as He died on a cross to set us free from the penalty our sins deserved, He used you that day to model true forgiveness. I wish I could say I forgave everyone that way. I'm ashamed to say I've kept people on the hook for a long time. Writing this book is helping me set them free.

Thank you for setting me free. I will remember the third grade as the year I learned about grace.

VII

Mrs. Asendorf

Dear Mrs. Asendorf,

It was mid-November when we met. The pretty fall leaves were gone, and winter was on its way. I was facing a winter in my own heart because we had just moved, and I was adjusting to a new school. The teacher I left behind was like the warm colors of the autumn leaves. In contrast, my new fourth-grade teacher seemed harsh and cold.

In search of a warm touch, I found refuge in the school health room. Just your gentle hands feeling my forehead provided the comfort I needed to continue to function. I came to you with a lot of stomach aches, but, truly, it was my heart that was hurting. We had moved from a Baltimore rowhouse to a house that sat by itself in Howard County. My father was proud. He finally had the house of his dreams. The same year, he also bought his own used-car business. To my father, the house and the car business were trophies validating his self-worth. He celebrated his success with alcohol. The real disease that caused my headaches and tummy aches was his alcoholism. Although my father was the alcoholic, all of us suffered from the disease. My mother dealt with her pain by using tranquilizers. Inventing pain to get your attention was one of the ways I dealt with mine.

The health room provided a temporary shelter for me. It was a place I could escape from a classroom of strangers who didn't understand me. I was an outsider who entered like a scared mouse. I was so nervous that I made others feel uncomfortable. Tears teetered at the edge of my eyes, ready to spill out at any moment. Your son, David, was in my class. He had a sensitive, compassionate nature rarely developed in children his age. I can see now that he was a product of your excellent role-modeling. He seemed to sense my struggles as I tried to adjust in a new situation. I could tell he understood just by the way he looked at me. Sometimes he tried to make things better with his dry sense of humor or a smile.

Pleasing my teacher seemed like an impossible task. I came to see you when I was weary from trying. Your personality was always the same: calm and steady, kind and compassionate. I felt I was living in a world where the rules kept changing. It was a relief to be in a place where things stayed the same.

My visits to the health room continued throughout fourth, fifth and sixth grades. Fifth grade was especially difficult. My mother, exasperated from trying to control my father's drinking, often gave up and tried to kill herself. Overdosing on her green medicine was the usual means of attempted escape. She went for days without moving from her bed. Sometimes, I came to school wondering if she would be alive when I got home. Other times, she resorted to more creative, melodramatic attempts to end her life. One day, she took off her shirt and stood in the cold garage, claiming she would get pneumonia and die. When it was just beginning to dawn on me that she wasn't really serious, the mother of a boy in my class killed herself. Suicide became a reality. The bewildered, worried look that boy shared with his little brother haunts me yet. I saw them standing on the front steps of the school, wondering why their mother had not come to pick them up as she had always done. After that, I lived in fear of losing my mother. I focused on the moments when I could see her as "good." It surprised both of us when I volunteered her to be the fifth-grade room mother. I thought she was wonderful as I watched her hands tying up treats in Halloween bundles. I was impressed that she was able to curl the orange ribbons with a scrape of the scissor blade.

My mother lived her life like the orange ribbons. She lived on the edge until she finally snapped and curled up. On at least two occasions she asked to be taken to "the nut house." Each time, she returned the same day, proclaiming she wasn't as crazy as "those other people." She wasn't crazy, but she was sick.

I wasn't sick, but I needed to come to your health room to feel better. The memory of your soft voice and your gentle touch continues to relieve the pain of the past. Now I have found the cure for the pain through my faith in Jesus. I can see He was there all along, taking care of me through people like you. Thank you for your tender care. It made a difference in my life.

VIII

Miss Pauline

Dear Miss Pauline,

How I wish I could mail this letter to heaven. I was saddened to hear that cancer claimed your life several years ago. However, I find comfort knowing that I will see you again. You walked so closely with God. I know you are with Him now.

I'm sure I never gave you more than a polite "thank you" in return for the many kind things you did for me. I was only a child, taking from you what I so desperately needed. Looking back, with the eyes of a grateful adult, I can see that you were a life line. Not only for me, but for my mother, as well.

We went to your house every time we ran out of something. It seemed that you always had whatever we needed. Our greatest blessing was your endless supply of patience. No matter what you were doing, you always stopped and listened. I can't imagine how my mother would have survived if you had not been there. Actually, you did much more than listen; you mothered her. My father and I were not much help when she was the one who was sick. You were always there during her recovery periods, bringing meals and changing bed linens. You were a true model of someone with a servant's heart. The Scripture says, "God will meet all your needs . . ." (Phil. 4:19). There is no doubt that He placed you next door to supply us with so much of what we were lacking.

I don't know how you had time to take care of us as well as your own family. You were a wonderful mother to your daughter. I remember you as a Girl Scout troop leader, cutting out felt animals for a project. As

I write this, I can see how much you influenced me. Some of my most rewarding experiences have been as a Brownie Scout leader.

I cannot help thinking of you every time I knit. You used to knit every night, making beautiful sweaters with intricate designs. One Christmas, I received a "Knitting for Barbie" kit. I couldn't wait for you to teach me how to read the directions so I could begin knitting a wardrobe for my beloved Barbie dolls. I can picture myself sitting beside you on your sofa as you taught me how to hold the needles. I was so impatient when you told me to rip out several rows to go back and pick up a slipped stitch. I can still hear your voice: "If it's worth doing, it's worth doing right."

I knit often now. It relaxes me. It reminds me of those days on your sofa in the security of your home. Since then, I've ripped out many woolen rows to go back and fix a mistake. The soft reminder has stayed with me: "If it's worth doing, it's worth doing right." Perhaps that is what my letter-writing is all about—going back to fix the mistakes in the buried stitches. I can't change the problems of the past, but I can change the way those problems affect my life. I can be "fixed." I truly believe that He who began a good work in me will complete it.

I spent so much of my life wishing I were your daughter. I even told some school friends at a church carnival that you were my mother. I spotted you walking with my mother and said, "There is my mother." When one of my friends inquired, "Which one?" I said, "The one with the glasses." That was you, Miss Pauline. I felt guilty I had lied, but the truth was that I wanted you, not her.

I felt she didn't want me, either. I had become

mouthy during my middle school years. Much of the fear that had plagued me as a small child had been replaced with anger.

You saw that mouthy, bratty side of me more than once. I was always surprised that you continued to make me my own tin of chocolate chip cookies every time you baked. You were consistently kind, even when I was undeserving.

Although I talked back, I was still the scared little girl who thought she was bad. My mother continued to have a great deal of control, although I fought to keep her from knowing. No wonder she came to you like a battered soldier. She was battle-weary. When she wasn't fighting my father, she was fighting me.

Even her repeated suicide attempts had developed a predictable pattern. She began with the intensity of a martyred saint, groaning out against injustice. Then she took just enough medication to knock herself out for about twenty-four hours. When she rose again, she would be rested and ready for another round of attacks on my father.

The first few times, I had feared she would never wake up. But after several years of the same scenario, I knew how the melodrama would unfold. It is no wonder I later excelled in acting. I had been learning the lines to survive on an alcoholic stage my entire childhood.

My mother had vowed to stop beating me the night our house caught on fire. She kept that vow until my sassy mouth rekindled the fire within her about four years later. I deserved discipline, but my mother was not equipped with the tools for good discipline. Her green medicine habit erased the boundaries. She always went too far. She pulled hair, pinched, kicked, took off her shoes, threw them, and then used them to beat me.

She stopped when she was tired. That is usually when she left and went to your house.

You never judged any of us, Miss Pauline. You just loved us. In your own way, you taught us about Jesus. You see, He did not live in us. Our hearts were too hard. We could not ask Him to come in. We were too busy guarding our hearts from each other.

Even though our hearts were hard, they still broke. You had what we needed to mend them. I didn't recognize Him then, but as I rip out the stitches and go back to the mistake, I can see Jesus lived in you. I can think of no greater goal than to be a mirror for Jesus. That is what you were, Miss Pauline—a reflection of Jesus.

You provided patience, an ear to listen, unmerited favor and love without condemnation. Thank you for everything we borrowed from you. How grateful I am that I, too, have found the Source that never runs out.

IX

Susan

My dear Susie,

As I watch my pen form the words on this page, I can't help but smile. I remember painstakingly trying to write straight up and down with big loops like you. Sitting behind you in junior high, I observed your penmanship and practiced diligently when I went home. I've been using your handwriting style ever since.

I had admired you from afar all through fourth and fifth grades. When the sixth grade classes did a re-enactment of the United Nations, I was down on the gym floor as Lebanon, but it seemed fitting that you were up on the stage as the United States.

Our paths finally came together when I joined your mother's Girl Scout troop. The first time I went to your house was to get more cookies to sell. I saw the family pictures on the mantel and thought your two older sisters looked like models. As I left that day, Ruth was just returning with a date. I was thrilled when he asked if I were her sister. I wished I was. I wished I lived in that cozy house with such kind people. I sold a lot of cookies that year. My greatest motivation was going back to your house to get more.

I wanted so badly to look like you. Do you remember when we both tried out for "The Littlest Angel?" We tried out on different days, but the people casting the part thought we were the same person. Neither one of us got the part (they said we were too tall) but my disappointment at not getting the part was overshadowed by the joy of being mistaken for you. Years later, when you went with me to register for college, someone asked if we were sisters. I felt I had finally "arrived." I look back in amusement at your reaction to all of this idol worship. You just laughed. In fact, you thought I was kidding.

I had you and your family on a pedestal. None of you claimed or pretended to be any more than you were. You merely welcomed me into your lives and invited me to be myself. I felt more at home in your house than I did in my own.

I remember many things about your home. Your mother saved the tin plates from TV dinners and used them again to freeze leftovers. She apologized profusely for serving one of her homemade TV dinners to me one evening. She didn't know I felt I had been invited to a banquet.

I loved the way you and your mother wrapped gifts. The paper always had small, dainty patterns that reflected your personality. I remember the box you had with bits and pieces of wrapping paper and ribbons. I have a box like that in my home now. Many times, I think of you when I'm wrapping a gift. You and your family were thoughtful, giving people. Every gift was wrapped with love. You brought me a gift in the hospital when I had my appendix taken out, a tiny little box with drawers for small treasures. I loved it, and I kept it for years. I would hold it in my hand and recapture the joy of opening each little drawer.

I can remember looking in your front window at you and your dad adding new fish to your fish tank. Looking in that window was like watching a Disney movie. When your father invited me to go with you to the fish store, I felt I had been given the role of the co-star.

Your father loved flowers. He was proud of his greenhouse. Do you remember the day he gave me one of his orchids? I will never forget it. I felt as if I had been given the Hope Diamond. Although the flower did not last, the love it represented still grows in my heart.

You used to know exactly what time your dad would be home from work. You ran to greet him with a kiss. Susan, I never knew when my dad was coming home or what condition he would be in. He rarely came home sober. His drunken behavior ranged from silly and lethargic to mean and defensive. In response, my mother's behavior ranged from total disgust to deep depression. I could never predict what would happen. I always feared the worst. On more than one occasion, the reality outweighed the fearful expectation. Once I felt so afraid that I picked up the phone to call the police. My father caught me and ripped the phone out of the wall. I felt as if I lived in a jungle of weeds. You may have mistaken our weeds for flowers because my father, my mother and I had learned to use our sense of humor as a cover-up. You found us entertaining. Although I have learned to laugh about much of my past, I was crying on the inside for years, a pitiful cry for approval and affirmation. Outwardly, we may have appeared to be a happy family; however, on the inside, the destructive seed of my father's alcoholism was producing a harvest of weeds. The weeds were choking our chances to grow and to be the real flowers God had designed us to be.

By the grace of God, I survived. He provided me with people like you so I would be able to recognize a real flower.

Thank you, Susie, for sharing your life with me. When I had no identity of my own, I shared yours. I spent four years of my young life wishing I were someone else. Although it is sad, I can't think of a better role model. It is only now that I am coming to peace with who I am. Part of the Great Commandment is to "love your neighbor as yourself" (Matt. 19:19). The only way I can love others with no strings attached is to love myself first.

I have always been so needy that my love for others has been motivated by the desire to be loved in return. Learning to love myself is allowing me to love others freely. I know who I am now. I have found my identity in Christ Jesus. It is my heart's desire that others see Him in me. I realize it was His love I saw in you and desired for myself. How happy I am that I can say I have accepted the ultimate gift. Like your gifts, it was wrapped in love. The person who thought we were sisters was right after all. We are sisters in Christ. I love you, my sister.

X

LINDSEY

My dear Lindsey,

For a thirteen-year-old, you drive a hard bargain. You made a deal with me: If I agreed to rent you a video game and buy you a lime slush, I could read your poem. Once I agreed to your terms and read the poem, I knew I had paid a small price for something quite valuable.

Dragons *by Lynn Smith*

I was ten
When we moved here
In a crystallized cocoon
of my books
and self-delusions
And the dragons swirled around me
But they could not reach me

I was eleven
When I started middle school
I broke out of my cocoon
only to find
A cruel world of laughter and hate
For someone they didn't understand
And the dragons found me
And tore my soul
into a thousand pieces
The only one to put me back together
my Rat

I was twelve
I could stand it no longer
I cried out my injustice
I learned from my mistakes

I made friends
And the dragons balked

I am thirteen
After three years of torture
I have friends
What would have made me cry
Now makes me laugh
And I have captured the dragons
with my pencil
and imprisoned them
on the still, lifeless paper

What you have done in the last three years is what I have been trying to do my whole life. I, too, have functioned in a cocoon of books and self-delusions. I, too, have been misunderstood. My soul has been torn into a thousand pieces. By the grace of God, He has put me back together. I've cried out my feelings of injustice, and He has provided friends that have become like family. The dragons have balked. As I write, I join you in capturing the dragons and imprisoning them on paper. My prayer is that when others read what I have written, they will recognize ways to capture their own dragons and be set free.

As I watch you grow and become the person God wants you to be, I marvel at His perfect design for our lives. I always pictured myself with a little daughter, dressed in pink, taking dancing lessons and playing with Barbie dolls. I realize that little girl is me, the little girl I always wanted to be. You are you. I've never been able to mold or shape you into my image. At times, I was frustrated. Now I look at you, and I rejoice. I see all that you are and all you can be. I am excited and proud that you are part of my life.

I wish I had written you the letter that was on my

heart the day you were born. You were a beautiful baby. I felt a love for you I had never felt before. I experienced a strong, protective instinct that almost scared me. Looking down at you, so helpless and beautiful, I felt at that moment I would be willing to kill anyone or anything that would threaten to hurt you. I did not realize I was capable of such strong and aggressive feelings.

Sometimes I would look at you in your bassinet and cry as I watched you sleep. You were so precious—you still are. If I could have made the world a perfect place for you, I would have.

Every hour, every minute, every thought was devoted to creating an exciting place for you to live. Even in your crib, pages were turned in books every five minutes so that, as you moved your tiny head, there was always something new for you to see. I rearranged your stuffed animals into little scenarios to greet you from your slumber. You were delighted with each new arrangement. The animals held everything in their furry paws from open books to plastic teacups. Everything was done in your honor, at times to extremes.

My previous experience as a first-grade teacher was probably your greatest handicap. We played endlessly with the alphabet. I taught you letters, sounds, blends and color words—all before you were three. I enjoyed being your teacher. You were such an eager learner. Like a sponge, you absorbed and retained everything. I wish I had been able to give you more than ABCs and color words. At the time, it was all I had to give. I could not relax and really enjoy your early childhood.

I was afraid to be a mommy. My life at your age was scary. The dragons of alcohol and drug abuse in my home swirled and attacked without mercy, like secret monsters. At first, I thought my mother was the dragon.

I can see now that she was a victim, just like me. We were caught in a vicious cycle of hurt.

My greatest fear has always been that I would hurt you. I know there have been times when I have. I overreacted when you got a B instead of an A in Reading on your first-grade report card. I should have understood that you were bored and trying to adjust to a new school. Instead, I took it as a personal affront because I had worked so hard teaching you to read.

I haven't been a perfect mother, Lynn, but by the grace of God, the cycle has been broken. At first, I used the role of a teacher as an alternative to being a mother. The dragons of my past deceived me into thinking I could never be a good mother. They were wrong. "I can do everything through him who gives me strength" (Phil. 4:13).

We still have your teen years ahead, puberty and menopause sharing the same roof. Not all of our days will be peaceful. We will face the conflicts all mothers and daughters encounter as they journey together. I am so grateful we both have captured our dragons on paper. We will not have to battle them on our paths. I have learned so much from you, my sweet daughter. You've made a difference in my life. I pray God directs me to make a positive difference in yours.

I love you, honey. I love being your mother.

XI

Jewel

Jewel honey,

I was so glad to see you at our high school reunion a few weeks ago. Even after twenty-five years, being with you felt the same as it did when we shared a seat on the bus and talked about boyfriends. I saved all the notes we wrote in religion class, each one about a different boy. My affections jumped from boyfriend to boyfriend like a game of leapfrog. Do you remember how I sat with Jeffrey and then switched seats when we got to Steve's stop? I loved it. My mother wanted me to marry Jeffrey. He was so studious, and he was planning to be a doctor. She told me he was good husband material. I thought he was boring, but really he was just mature beyond his years. I ended up marrying someone just like him. I feel lucky. I'm sure whoever got Jeffrey is lucky, too. Sometimes boring really means peaceful.

Peace was something I did not know during my high school years. Quiet times at my house were like the eye of a hurricane—brief periods of rest before the next crisis. As much as I loved my father, I could not trust him to be the father I needed. I think most of my hopping from boyfriend to boyfriend was my way of seeking the male attention I was lacking. I made sure I was the one to break up first to avoid any possibility of being rejected. My greatest fear was that my father would reject me as he had my brother.

I had little remorse for the broken hearts of boys. I collected them like charms on a bracelet. You were always amazed at my boldness and used to tell me that I had a lot of nerve. I definitely had too much ego. As long as I had a boyfriend and a best friend, I felt validated. The boyfriends changed constantly; you remained my best friend.

As the oldest girl in a family of five, you had learned to be responsible and considerate of others. In contrast, I was an only child who had become a master of manipulation. I still cannot understand why you put up with me. I must have been the bad little girl you always wanted to be, blurting out the things you never dared say. Your laughter encouraged me, and I was never at a loss for new material. I derived great pleasure playing devil's advocate in Sister Brendan Marie's religion class. I said things just to pull her chain. Sometimes it was just an act. Unfortunately, I developed some destructive talking habits. I still struggle to keep a guard on my mouth.

My parents adored you, and we took you on our summer vacations to Ocean City. You and I stole squirt guns from a gift shop and spent our evenings squirting cute boys as we strolled the boardwalk. I thank God we were not caught. My mother would have been furious. My father would have been crushed. He gave us spending money and money for meals every day. We skipped meals and ate banana splits. One time, we ordered dinner, ate it and left without paying. I am so ashamed of this now; however, I felt no remorse at the time. I think I shut off the valve leading to my conscience. Most of my childhood, I felt guilty and ashamed. Being free enough to be bad felt good.

Unlike you and most of the girls in our Catholic high school, I was not accustomed to nuns. I had expected all the nuns to be kind and as beautiful as Audrey Hepburn. I had idolized the young nun who gave me instructions for my First Holy Communion in second grade, and I thought they all would be like her. Not so. We had a real garden variety at Keough High.

Remember Sister Stansia? She was the one who told us not to wear patent leather shoes because they would reflect our underwear. She was the home-economics teacher and struggled to teach us how to sew. You loved it, but I hated it. Images of my mother sitting grim-faced behind a sewing machine evoked feelings of fear and hostility. I never knew when she would rise up to chase me, scissors in hand. I hated to try on her horrible creations as she pinned seams and hems. I paid a high price for a scream when a pin stuck me instead of the material.

It is hard to remember my mother doing anything other than cooking, sewing, beating or screaming. My elementary school years had finally been better. I thought it was because I was better, but adolescence prompted the rebellion of the good little girl.

Much of my fear was replaced with anger. I learned to talk back and lived to regret the consequences. My mother was a brutal fighter. She pinched, kicked and pounded. There were bruises all over my body. I lived for the change-of-uniform days, when we switched from our white crew socks to knee socks, which covered my legs. I rarely went without my sweater to cover my arms.

Do you remember the day in ninth grade that the home health care nurse visited Sister Stansia's class? She asked for a volunteer patient to demonstrate a bed bath. I volunteered you. When you turned red with embarrassment, the nurse told me to come instead. I deserved that one. However, the embarrassment I suffered when she told me to take off my sweater and when she pulled down my knee socks was unbearable. Without thinking, the poor woman blurted out words that still bring shame: "Who is beating you?"

I made a glib remark about being clumsy. Later in private, I told her my father drank a lot, and he beat me. I still feel bad about lying. Other girls in our school had fathers who drank with my father. Although never acknowledged, we all kept one another's secrets.

Nothing was ever said to my parents, but something changed in me that day. I vowed I would not submit to those beatings again. The next time my mother came after me, I hit her back. It surprised me as much as it did her. As a child, I had never been able to hit anyone.

Shocked, she looked at me and said, "You hit me!"

I looked back and said, "Do you just expect me to take it?" I expected her to kill me. Instead, she turned away, and she never hit me again.

I felt no pride in my victory, only fear of my own power. It was about this time that my mother stopped taking the green medicine that was causing her irrational behavior. How tragic that I punished myself and hated my mother when the green medicine was the real enemy.

I began to change after that. I guess striking my mother was the start of reconnecting that valve to my conscience. I didn't want to be bad. I was afraid of the bad girl inside, and I wanted to be good.

Back then, "anorexia" was not the buzzword it has become. I literally tried to starve my body to look like a little girl again. I wrapped an ace bandage around my chest to make me look flat-chested. I only felt attractive when I could see my bones poking through my skin. I even tried to dress like a little girl. My mother, minus the drugs, had become more reasonable. She finally allowed me to choose patterns and material for my homemade dresses. I chose puffy-sleeved dresses with pinafores. At last, I was playing the part I always wanted to play—the role of a good little girl. I must have looked ridiculous, but it didn't matter. I was happier.

Drama was one of my greatest outlets. I grieved that I was too tall to be one of the younger children in the school production of *The Sound of Music*. However, I was thrilled to get the part of Louisa. I was the only sophomore with a main part. Several people at our twenty-fifth reunion remembered me as the star. What an illusion! It was a miracle I got a part at all, considering I can't sing or dance.

I was thrilled when I got to sing a few lines as a little girl in the Junior Talent Show. You were a member of a barber shop quartet and wore a black construction paper mustache. You just wanted your part to be over. I wanted my part to last forever. I loved that school stage more than any place on earth then. I remember every line from the excerpt of "Joan of Arc" I used as my audition for the drama club.

The drama club was an important part of my high school script. The director, Sister Joanita, was the most beautiful woman I had ever known. She looked like Grace Kelly in a black habit. She was encouraging to me as a member of her drama team. I was always thrilled when she took extra time to coach me. I couldn't wait until my sophomore year, when I would be in her English class. I was devastated when she didn't return in the fall. There was a rumor that she had tuberculosis. When I came home and told my mother, I was horrified at her response. She said, "If she has tuberculosis, she's going to die." I sat on my bed and cried for hours.

Sister Joanita did return. She looked smaller and more frail, yet even more beautiful. I cherished every moment with her. Many nights, I wrote her long, emotional letters, sharing my innermost thoughts. I saved them all in a box, afraid to give them to her. My mother said I had a crush on her.

At the end of our junior year, Sister Joanita announced she was leaving. She and another nun were going to get an apartment and teach in public school. The Catholic Church was going through a transition. It caused quite a stir when the nuns changed to modified habits and let some hair show. As much as I hated to see her leave, I admired her determination to blaze a new trail as an "undercover" nun.

As part of the hippie generation, all of us were ready to throw out tradition and save the world. Sister Joanita was my personal hero, a major influence in my decision to become a nun. I tried to convince myself and everyone else that it was a call from God, but I don't believe my heavenly phone was even connected. You were supportive after you recovered from the shock.

Being the girl who was going to be a nun had its own notoriety. The parish priest preached a whole sermon on a letter I wrote to the Catholic Review.

I spent the summer of my junior year reading about the lives of saints and waiting for visions. I wanted to be "holy" by my senior year. I spent a lot of time in the chapel that fall, writing prayers and leaving them on the altar. I had a new part to play, and I played it well. I even convinced myself that it was real. I believe now that I was still looking for a way to believe I was a good little girl.

My father, who never liked my boy-crazy ways, was thrilled. My mother could barely stomach the phone calls from friends and neighbors congratulating her on her daughter's decision. She opposed the idea from the start. She felt God had played a dirty trick on her. Why take her only daughter? My aunt had five children. "Let one of them become a nun or a priest," she said. Her biggest complaint was she had spent a fortune straightening my teeth and getting me contact lenses. If she had known I was going to waste my life away as a nun, she would have saved her money. The more she tried to persuade me I was making a mistake, the more determined I became. It is painful to believe that I would enter the convent just to rebel against my mother; however, in retrospect, I can see that rebellion was a factor.

Children rebel in different ways. Ironically, I can

remember the woman who raised her eyes, clucked her tongue and separated Steve and me because we were dancing too closely at a Catholic Youth Organization dance in our freshman year. Ultimately, I became a nun, and her daughter had to get married because she was pregnant.

I can't judge her. Being a mother is hard. The most difficult challenge is to allow our daughters to become who they are and not who we want them to be. It's easy to push too hard. My daughter will start high school this fall. She is the same age you and I were when we met. One of my greatest prayers for her is to meet a friend who will mean to her what you have meant to me.

Although my decision to become a nun separated our paths, you were there when I needed you. Part of me died when Sister Joanita's murdered body was found three months after she was listed as missing. I don't think I ever cried so much. At the funeral, you and I tore a tissue in half and shared it. I felt you shared my broken heart, too.

Jewel, our friendship has always seemed so one-sided. I did all the taking, and you did all the giving. I don't remember ever being there for you when it was your turn to hurt. You never took your turn. Was I so selfish that I never gave you a turn?

Thank you, my dear friend, for letting me take so much from you. I still have the pink crystal rosary you gave me when I entered the convent. Each bead sparkles like a jewel and reminds me to count the many blessings I received from your friendship. Just as your name suggests, you were a gem, a rare find in an adolescent setting. I realize that you allowed me to believe I was the one who sparkled.

I thank my God every time I remember you. You are indeed a precious jewel.

XII

Eileen

Dear Eileen,

Twenty-four years ago, when you and I were in the convent together, I never pictured myself married, with two children, writing you a letter like this. I wanted to be a nun with my whole heart. For years, I had been pinning pillowcases on my head and twirling around with my arms outstretched like Julie Andrews. I had everything to look the part except the voice. I played the part well. Haley Mills (*The Trouble With Angels* and Sally Field (*The Flying Nun*) had nothing on me. They had their antics recorded for a television audience; I performed live every day, but not all of my audiences found me amusing. Gratefully, you did. You said I was "refreshing." That term has been used to describe me on more than one occasion; it usually follows something stupid that I've said or done.

The convent is in Baltimore, Maryland, one street over from Memorial Stadium. When the Chapel windows were open during the spring months, calls like "strike one, ball two" punctuated our Hail Marys and Our Fathers. I was the youngest member of the community and the only postulant. Six months later, when you entered, I was elated that there would be another rookie on the team. Eight years older, with education and life experience, you had a desire to know and serve the Lord. I, on the other hand, had spent my life in the dugout and was just grateful I had found my way to home base.

I think you were the only one amused at my welcome for you. I rolled a huge (everything we had was the industrial size) roll of white paper towels down the hallways leading to your room. The white welcome carpet led to your bed, which was turned down and probably short-sheeted. A big doll dressed in a nun habit was waiting for you on the bed, rosary and prayer book in hand. I appreciated your support when I was admonished for wasting paper. You said, "They missed the whole point." I think they missed a lot of my points. I'm not sure why—I was always willing to explain.

You didn't feel the need to explain much. You just said what you felt. You were so smart, Eileen. You had a master's degree in counseling, and your mind was ready for greater challenges than my just-turned-twenty-year-old brain. I was only trying to think of a way to look holy and still be fun. I think you were seeking ways to become holy and make sense of the mundane ritual-type lifestyle of the Order. I can see now that you were truly searching for meaning, trying to discern between true obedience and blind ignorance. No wonder you found me refreshing. I couldn't think that deeply. I didn't know what I was searching for, other than a place where I could belong and appear holy.

I have to admit the holy look was not always easy. Remember my pink fuzzy slippers I wore to evening chapel? I continued to look serene and smile meekly when the older sisters turned around to see who was laughing. They had no idea I was pointing my furry foot in the aisle every time we chanted "Glory be to the Father."

Before you entered, I set my alarm for 5 A.M. to plug in my electric curlers. Somehow I managed to curl my hair and apply my secret supply of eyeliner and blush before I went to morning prayer. I was usually late—beautiful, but late. One day, I left an electric curler in the back of my hair. No doubt, the life spans of several of those sainted women were shortened when that heavy curler hit the wooden bench.

My hair was a constant source of controversy with the sisters. I was amused when I went back to visit after twenty years that many of you were still doing imitations of me flipping my hair over my shoulder. During those days of waist-length hair, no one seemed to regard it as a laughing matter. Usually, there would be a chorus of gasps as my hair fell forward while I was lighting candles for Mass. Those poor elderly sisters thought they were about to see a rerun of *Joan of Arc,* minus the saintly cause. Having long hair to rebel against conformity was about as deep as my cause went.

Remember our private classes with Sister Bonaventure? On the first day, when she pulled out her Bible, I boldly pronounced, "I know all that stuff." You just cracked up and said that we might learn a few new things. How sad that we didn't, other than techniques on how to avoid being lulled to sleep by the sound of her voice. She soon grew frustrated by our lack of response. We were given a small book and instructed to read it by the following week. When the day arrived, you asked if I had read it. "Of course not," I replied. You laughed and confessed you never opened the cover, either. When Sister Bonaventure asked if we had read the book, you were honest and told her you just hadn't had the time. I, of course, lied right to her face. "Oh yes, sister, I read the whole thing," I said in my most angelic voice. I expected her to praise me and then lecture on for the next hour while I basked in her approval. Instead, she asked me to please share what I had learned. "Oh," I replied, "actually, I only had time to read the title." At that response, we were both dismissed. We laughed all the way back to the novitiate.

Later, we were called into Sister Catherine's office. She was disgusted. Sister Bonaventure had taught novices for years and was well-loved and respected by all. She was unaccustomed to young sisters who thought they knew it all and would come unprepared to her class and (she shot a look my way) would lie about it. Sister Bonaventure refused to teach us another lesson. Our classes were terminated. I hung my head in shame. You, in contrast, replied "Good. It was a boring waste of time, anyway." You walked away with no remorse; I went to my room and wrote a long letter of apology. However, if our hearts were judged on true sincerity that day, I'm sure your heart was the one that was true.

My true motive was to seek approval and attention. Years after I left the convent and admitted those motives to myself, I was disgusted with myself. I figured that the sisters who remained felt the same way about me. It was twenty years before I renewed contact. How surprised I was to be greeted with such love.

I believe with all my heart that my two years in the convent were part of God's plan for my life. I may have been under the illusion that I entered the convent to serve God, but the real truth was He provided a place for me to be served with huge helpings of love.

For the first time in my life, I could go to sleep at night and not worry about my father coming in drunk and my mother responding hysterically. I learned to trust the sisters. Much of my immature acting out was a way of getting from the sisters what had been lacking in my home. I felt free enough to be "naughty." I was like a little girl surrounded by grandmothers. The craziness of some of the rules and the boredom of the routine provided the feelings of safe boundaries I had never known in my alcoholic home. The boundaries in my home changed constantly. I rarely tested authority because I lived in fear. Living in the convent was an escape from that fear; testing the boundaries became a childish game. I was always admonished with a lot of love and grace, although at times, I pushed to the point of exasperation. When the neighborhood children rang the doorbell for the third time on Silent Sunday to see if Sister Michelle could come out to play, Mother General emphatically said, "Enough is enough!"

For a while, the convent provided a secure place to have my needs met. I feel each sister gave me something special. It gives me pleasure now as I find the little seeds that were planted in the convent have grown in my heart. I have been able to give to others that which was given to me.

Sister Giles will always remain one of my favorite benefactors. She asked me to read to her every day because her eyes were failing. We read Thomas Merton's biography. I can't remember the contents of the book, but the memory of the feeling remains warm. Sister Giles used the book as a means of ministering to me under the guise of a service to her. I treasure the letters and cards she sent me after I left the convent. Do you remember how they used to cut out the inside of old greeting cards and use them for note cards? I even have a few where pictures of flowers are pasted over the old signature.

I found my own way to recycle. Cleaning out the closets, I found many treasures, my favorite being the boxes of tiny whips with knotted ropes. I can't believe they used those to chastise themselves. The day I found them, I also found some old Generalate stationery. I typed you a forged letter from the Mother General explaining the readoption of the scourging practice. You were given strict and specific instructions to beat yourself every Friday night at a designated time. Knowing by the typing errors the letter was from me, you decided to play along. At the designated time, you went into your room, hit your desk, and moaned in distress. I burst into your room to save you from my joke, only to be greeted by your laughter.

We laughed together a lot, Eileen. It was the way we survived when things got too tough. We learned that coughing in chapel would bring Sister Agnes to our rescue. She would send us to bed and bring us hot lemonade and whiskey.

We made up nicknames for all those people in that religious formation class we attended. Remember "Dagwood"? The poor, kind priest never knew we were laughing at him. The class was held in a seminary in Washington, D.C. Remember how cute those two seminarians were? (Thoughts like that did not prepare me for a vow of celibacy.) I especially liked eating lunch in their refectory. We were the only women in a room full of young men.

I'll never forget our refectory. The crucifix on the central wall had a Jesus almost as big as I was. It was realistic with the nails, blood and crown of thorns—quite an appetizing centerpiece to see while eating.

When I went back to visit, I saw it was still there, but the hardwood floors were covered with carpet. I had mopped that floor many times. The first time I tried to shine it with the industrial-size buffer, that statue of Mary, the one with the crown of stars, almost went flying off the pedestal in the hall. I saw my whole life flash before my eyes when she started to tilt.

I wasn't very good at steering anything. Remember pushing those huge food carts for dinner? We had to stand beside them while we prayed and then lift off the big metal lids. I usually caused a scene, trying to roll my cart through the door without hitting it.

I have to admit, I'm not much better at driving a

car. I hate to drive. I finally learned after I left the convent, when I got my first teaching job. You were not pleased that I could not help you drive the older sisters hither and yon. You despised those trips, especially when Sister Cynthia wouldn't tell you where you were going, only how to get there.

Sister Cynthia was quite a character with her secrets. Everyone knew (but no one ever told her that we knew) she dyed those front locks of hair. I can still picture her small frame walking with great purpose down the convent halls, her dyed red bangs proudly poking from under her black veil. I made sure I stayed on her good side since she was in charge of the candy cupboard. It was under lock and key and constant surveillance. Every evening, Sister Cynthia brought out some chocolates for "recreation time." The chocolates were of high quality as they were generally gifts from lay people who thought that giving expensive chocolates to nuns assured them a seat in heaven. I just made sure I sat near the box.

I never saw you in there knitting bandages for the lepers during recreation time, Eileen. You said you had enough chit-chat while driving all day. You were usually in the chapel, communicating with the Lord. I was stuffing candy in my mouth and knitting crooked leper bandages with chocolate fingerprints. I don't think I ever finished a whole bandage, but I'm sure I ate a whole box of candy. I made lots of deals with Sister Cynthia. On the side, I cleaned her classroom, made bulletin boards, or anything else she desired for extra chocolate. I never knew when she would pay me; everything with her was a secret. When I would least expect it, I would find chocolates wrapped in napkins pushed under my bedroom door.

During our second year, no longer postulants, we became novices. We chose the song "There's Got to Be a Morning After" from *The Poseidon Adventure* as our theme song. It was a movie about survivors on a sunken ship. I think we were hoping to survive ourselves.

Instead of navy blue, we were allowed to wear grey, the official color of the habit. You used to wear sophisticated little numbers by Jonathan Logan. You still had worldly connections. I got my mother to make me pinafore-type jumpers. Cute was still a priority. In addition to looking cute, I quickly discovered that looking busy was also to my advantage. If we weren't busy, the sisters always found something for us to do. You were generally stuck driving; my greatest service was cleaning. I was in charge of the bathrooms. You rolled your eyes when I scrubbed in between the tiles with a toothbrush.

The sisters liked me to stand on chairs to get the high places. Sometimes I didn't mind. Often they rewarded me with presents that ranged from holy cards to more recycled greeting cards. My favorite was a quilt made from a Raggedy Ann bed sheet someone donated to the Franciscan Center. Sister James made it for me. However, some days I was tired (we got up at an ungodly hour) or just plain lazy. I didn't always want to do extra chores, presents or not. I discovered that if I wore an apron and carried a can of Pledge and a rag, they thought I was busy. I could slip over to the west side of the building, which consisted of three halls of empty bedrooms, to take an afternoon nap in a different bed each day so they could never find me.

Recently, I found some prayer journals I kept during my two years as a nun. I believe I was playing hide and seek with God also. I wanted Him to find me, looking holy, being a good nun and doing good works. I wanted to hide all the bad parts. I believed I was a bad person, and everything good I did was an act. Deep down, I longed to be good and have a holy relationship with God. I saw those qualities reflected in the eyes of so many of the nuns, but I felt as if I never really measured up.

One evening, you found me crying and talked to me until late into the night. I was honest with you that night, Eileen. There was no costume, no play-acting; I was searching for me, for God and for purpose. You listened, you validated, and you encouraged. You couldn't fix it, but you helped me.

Shortly after that night, I was transferred to New York. The security of forty-two grandmothers was replaced with the dynamics of living with five women in various stages of menopause. I feel as if I was in the wrong place at the wrong time.

The house superior was trying to define her role. It was difficult to find the balance between respecting the older tradition and moving with the times. The entire Catholic Church was experiencing the pain of transition. At the time, I saw many of her decisions as inconsistent. At every conversation, I felt she understood and agreed with me, yet at times, I felt her actions betrayed me. I lacked the maturity to understand her position. I look back now with eyes of grace. I pray she remembers me with grace also.

As difficult as the move was for me, I loved my role in the church school. I worked in the first grade and as director for the eighth grade production of "Godspell."

Also, I felt great love and acceptance from the families there in the largely Italian parish. They spoiled me. The nuns took turns cooking, but I wasn't a good cook. (Do you remember the summer in Baltimore they assigned me to work in the kitchen with Sister Arnold? I lasted two weeks before she told me and everyone else it was not working.) Anyway, the Italian mamas of the parish provided the meal every time it was my turn to cook.

I also felt encouragement and support from the Monsignor and the three priests in the rectory next door. The youngest priest looked like Chad Everett. The superior was worried because we spent so much time together. I did have a little crush, but he was twelve years older than I was. Thirty-three seemed old back then. He was, however, the closest person to my age. I talked to him often because he was the only one I felt understood me. Most of our conversations were spent expressing frustrations. I had stopped playing the little girl games. I desired with my entire heart to be a good nun. I couldn't figure out what that meant in the eyes of the sisters; whatever it was, I wasn't it.

I chose to leave the convent the day after the eighth-grade play, feeling like a failure, and went back to the motherhouse for a retreat that summer. Although the sisters were kind, I felt like an outcast. I hardly talked to anyone, even to you. With the notion forming in my mind that I should take a leave of absence, I arranged to talk to Sister Christine. She had been there from the first time I started visiting the convent as a junior in high school. Only four years older than I, she had nevertheless watched many young nuns come and go. I could hardly face her because I had promised her when I entered that I would never leave. I knew by this time that I could not keep my promise. I asked for an indefinite leave of absence.

Twenty-two years have passed since I left the convent. Christine herself left after being a nun for more than twenty years. Like myself, she is happily married to a Baptist. Both of us have found being a nun is not the only way to love Jesus with all your heart, mind and soul. Neither of us regrets the time we spent as Franciscan nuns. I spent two; she spent twenty-two. For both of us, it was a part of our spiritual journeys.

I will be forever grateful it was part of mine.

Eileen, you were such an important person to me. You were so real. You made me want to be real, too. You never made me sweat because of what I wasn't. You made me thirst for what I could be. I couldn't do it back then because I didn't really know how to tap the Source of the living water.

I was trying so hard to earn that which is freely offered. You knew the fountain all along. That is why you were the one who was truly "refreshing." Thank you, my wonderful sister. You little rebel—you turned out to be a great nun. Before long, I hope to visit your retreat house in Maryland. You are the hope of the Catholic Church.

XIII

Dr. Freshour

Dear Dr. Freshour,

Do you remember the first letter I wrote to you? It was about twenty-two years ago, desperate scribbling on the back of a test paper. In essence, it was a suicide note. I sat in your reading education classroom at the University of South Florida, staring at the words on your test paper. They stared back, reminding me that I was unprepared. At lunch that day, a boy I had been dating gave me the classic let's-just-be-friends speech for dessert. It was too hard to swallow. Once again, I was a stupid, worthless failure. I turned the paper over and began to write. I cannot remember anything I said to you, other than, "I just want to die." I wrote until enough time had passed that others were turning in their papers and leaving. I handed you my paper and headed for my dorm room.

I opened the top drawer of my dresser where I kept a shoebox full of the medicine my mother had given me for every imaginable ailment. Some were over-the-counter, others were prescription samples, and others were pills in baggies with labels listing symptoms. I wished at that point that I could find one that said "guaranteed to kill you." Instead, I took every pill I had. It was not a ploy for attention. I honestly wanted to die.

I was furious to find myself alive in the University Hospital. A nurse struggled to hold me down as I tried to run and jump out the window. I hated the fact that my attempt to die had failed. The fact was I hated myself.

I had come to the University of South Florida in August with a unique set of baggage. I had just left the convent in May; in June, I moved to Melbourne,

Florida, where my parents had relocated. I was scared to death. Most students face transition pains of leaving home and living in a dorm. Try leaving a convent and then being thrust into a university atmosphere. I was without a script. I had no idea how to play the part.

I had completed my freshman year in a small community college before entering the convent. Then the sisters had assumed the cost while I completed my sophomore year at Loyola College in Baltimore. However, nothing had prepared me for a state university setting and its challenges.

My parents had not planned on having to support me and put me through college; therefore, they were unprepared. Also, it would take a year to establish residence, so the tuition costs were tripled. I managed to get a loan and a college work-study job, and my parents covered my room and board for the first year. I had given all my clothes away before I became a nun, so I had no clothes other than nun habits when I left Baltimore. My parents bought me a few basics to start school, yet I still had that insecure feeling that I didn't look like everyone else.

It was important for me to fit in. Deep down, I knew I didn't, so I overcompensated the best I could. I tried to act cool. That was never an act I had been able to play successfully, but I gave it a try. I drank at the beer parties, spiced my language with four-letter words and tried to be funny. To my surprise, it had seemed to be working, at least with the girls on my hall.

I lived in the only coed dorm, which meant there was a hall for males and a hall for females and a locked door in between. One night during a party, as we mingled in the halls, one boy who had caught my eye earlier approached me to talk. I was flattered that he noticed me and floored when I realized how much he had noticed. He told me he had been watching me and knew that something was not quite right. He said he just didn't believe I was the person I was pretending to be. I will never forget the look on the poor boy's face when I started to cry. I'm sure in his wildest dreams he would never have imagined that he had just picked up a girl who had studied to be a nun.

We started to date after that night. I became dependent upon him, feeling that he was the only one on the entire campus who really knew who I was. At first, I think he was intrigued; as time went on, I think he felt drained. I can't say that I loved him or that he broke my heart; he just validated the feelings of worthlessness within me when he rejected me. Growing up in a home with alcoholism and drug abuse set the stage for a rehearsal of lies telling me that I wasn't good enough. I became a nun because it provided a costume and a role to play, a role that could convince others and myself that I was good. The part got too hard. I had to give it up, and I left feeling disappointed and dejected. Feeling insecure on the college stage, I tried to play a new role. The one person who had seen through the act and seemed to be interested in the real me had turned and discarded me. I couldn't play anymore. I just wanted to die.

After I passed out from the pills, my roommate found me and called for emergency help. Later, when you found my letter, you gave it to a professor in the guidance department, who called me later that week. Thank you, Dr. Freshour, for caring about me. I remember you as a kind man. I appreciated the tenderness I found in your eyes when I began coming back to class.

I frightened the nurse when I struggled to reach for the window. I cried so much as I begged her to let me die that I made her cry, too. The counselor who saw me that day, on the other hand, had no intention of crying. Dr. Lilly Blau spoke with a harsh German accent. She confronted me and demanded to know why I was seeking so much attention. I cried at first, until her relentless accusations made me angry. I felt like a pot about to boil over. The words began to bubble so fast I can't remember what I said. I must have gone on for hours. At the time, I was in denial about the alcoholism and drug abuse in my home. I could only communicate that helpless feeling of trying so hard and never being good enough—at home, in the convent and now at school. I shouted at the end of my tirade, "And that's why I wanted to die!" For the first time, Lily smiled and then she laughed. She told me anyone who had that much anger had enough life in them to live. I couldn't explain why, but when I left her, I felt better.

I was required to have weekly counseling because of my suicide attempt. It was helpful. Between the counseling and the affirmation I received from my professors, I began to claim some feelings of self-worth.

My work-study job was in the Fine Arts Department, where I enjoyed the artistic temperament of the students and faculty. I began dating a student from the Music Department, whose gentle spirit was exactly what I needed.

Becoming a resident assistant in the dorm was another uplifting experience. Knowing how hard it can be, I found joy in helping others adjust to college. I went on to become an assistant resident instructor.

My intern teaching was one of the most encouraging boosts to my self-esteem. Dr. Purdom, my supervising professor, was an excellent mentor. His feedback was positive and specific, creating within me a desire to strive higher. I loved teaching. At last, I found a place where I felt successful.

After graduation, I stayed in school to get a master's degree. Partly due to your influence, I considered reading education. I loved teaching reading more than any other subject and feel you gave me a strong foundation. But I chose guidance counseling because it pulled my heart strings. I knew how much talking things out helped me. I wanted to help others.

In the end, I never pursued a counseling job; I preferred teaching. I now realize part of my need to help others was a way to try to fix in others that which was broken in me. I know now where those feelings of being so desperate originated. To end the pain, I would have been willing to die. Writing that letter to you twenty-two years ago was the first step in a journey of finding myself.

I praise God that the search for myself eventually led me to my Savior, Jesus Christ. God has had a perfect plan for me all along because of the grace of His Son. At last, I am good enough.

I believe you were part of the plan, Dr. Freshour. Your kindness and quiet sensitivity allowed me to cry out for the help I so desperately needed.

Thank you for being there.

XIV

Becky

Dear Becky,

The first time I saw you was a day of firsts. It was my first day of teaching first grade, on the first day of school. I had slept in my electric curlers, hoping for some body in my long, straight brown hair, but the September humidity quickly dashed those hopes. It hung limply over the puffy sleeves of my new dress. I had bought it because I thought the small checked pattern and full skirt made me look like a teacher. Actually, it made me look like Laura Ingalls Wilder. On more than one occasion, the students and their parents told me I looked like that girl from "The Little House on the Prairie." I bet no one ever told you that, Becky. You looked like Farrah Fawcett. Your blonde hair was always perfectly fashioned, every flip and twirl in place. You pulled every outfit together with the flair of a model. You knew how to apply your eye makeup just right, with never a smudge or a smear. All the little girls in your class wanted to grow up to look just like you.

Sometimes when people look so perfect, they are mistaken for snobs. This opinion is usually biased by the self-esteem of the beholder. Considering that I suffered from a lack of self-esteem, I fell prey to this misconception. Laura Ingalls Wilder did think Farrah Fawcett was stuck-up. Who would have ever thought the two would become roommates? I certainly never imagined such a scenario because I already had a roommate.

I had been married for a little more than a year when I started teaching. I felt lucky to be married to Robert, a man who was tall, dark and handsome. We met during my senior year of college when both of us were employed as housing counselors. He was on the soccer team, a big fish in a little pond of on-campus residents. I couldn't believe that I hooked him. I wasn't a big fish; however, I was a rare fish, a nun on leave of absence from the convent. I had decided after my first semester of graduate school that I would go back to the convent. The decision meant giving up my job as an assistant resident instructor, and the news quickly spread through the network in the dorm community. Robert was especially intrigued and asked me about it at a hall dance. We met every day after that evening and never ran out of things to talk about.

Many of our discussions revolved around religious issues. His mother was Jewish, and his father was Catholic. He had lived the first ten years of his life in South America with his father's family. Although his mother had converted, and he, his brother and two sisters had been baptized, they were not accepted well in the Catholic community. They faced enormous criticism because of his mother's Jewish origin. His father was strict and cruel, an abusive husband and father. Robert's mother divorced him and moved back to the states with his brother and sisters. Robert was forced to stay with his father for almost a year until she could gain his custody. He suffered greatly during the time of separation. To his father, he was merely a pawn kept to punish his mother. He described times of not having enough to eat; yet, his real hunger was for the arms of his mother, whom he adored. His mother later married the principal of the local elementary school, a Jewish man. Although he was also strict, and Robert initially rebelled his authority, he later formed a loving, respectful relationship and considered this man his "real" father.

Cords of bitterness toward his birth father were

tangled tightly with that of anger toward Catholicism. Relentlessly, he questioned my decision of commitment to the Catholic Church. The questions he asked were penetrating. At one point, I broke into tears of frustration, realizing I had no answers to some of his probes. The Catholic Church was my security blanket; becoming a nun was the way to wear that blanket as a badge of courage. His questions lifted that blanket and exposed the vulnerable young girl who was hovering beneath it.

With a sensitivity and a charm all his own, Robert made me believe he loved the girl under the blanket. I fell in love with him in a way I had never before experienced. Thoughts of him consumed me morning, noon and night. He seemed to feel the same. It was obvious to everyone who saw us. We became an on-campus love story: Romeo and Juliet, Bridget and Bernie, the girl who was going to be a nun and the Jewish soccer star. Although I still held tightly to the Catholic blanket, I gave up the chance to wear it as a habit. I terminated my leave of absence and made a final break with the Franciscan sisters in Baltimore.

I went home for Christmas, eager to tell my parents about Robert. My mother was relieved to know that her only child was not going to waste away in a convent. However, she was not as elated as I had anticipated. I quickly learned why. My father had become a bitter, distant man. Although it was Christmas, he wanted no display of happiness. I always played Christmas albums by Andy Williams and Robert Goulet. He ordered the music to be shut off and the records put away, threatening to break them all.

I had been raised in a home with all the trappings of codependency. I had played the role as my parents' counselor on many occasions; however, I had never seen this reaction from my father. As we talked, he told me he had no love for my mother, and he wanted to leave. He looked me straight in the eye and told me he wished he could get in a car and drive as far away as possible and never look back.

My first impulse was to try to fix the situation. It had been my impossible dream for years; however, now I had one semester of graduate counseling courses behind me. I had no idea I would pay a bitter price that day. My amateur counseling brought me information I wish to this day I could erase forever. It is painful to recall the questions I asked and more painful to recall the answers. I asked my father if he had ever been with other women. He looked at my mother, who hung her head. He looked back at me and said two words that stabbed my heart like a knife: "Yes, many."

I was in shock, Becky. I thought I knew everything. Later that night, as I talked to my mother, I realized how little I knew. Bit by bit, I was able to fit the pieces together. I remembered the face of a woman he had in our house when I came home from Girl Scout camp the time my mother was out of town. I felt like a fool for being so naïve. I was disgusted and revolted at the sight of my father. For perhaps the first time, I had some empathy for my mother. I had always thought she was the difficult one in the marriage and had been the cause of his drinking.

For a writing literacy exam, I had written an essay titled, "My Father, the Man I Most Admire." I had mailed the rough draft to my father earlier that fall. He cherished it and had saved it in his desk drawer. I tore through the papers in the drawer until I found it, and I ripped it to shreds. I have many memories of crisis-filled Christmases, but this was one of the worst.

I left the day after Christmas to spend the remainder of the holiday with Robert and his family in Miami. I had a wonderful time. I saw only what I wanted and needed to see. Looking back, knowing what I know now, I realize I didn't see things the way they were. I needed perfection; I saw perfection. Robert was perfect, his family was perfect, and I, with all my imperfection, was lucky to be able to share in their lives.

The "perfect" formula I just described always results in disappointment. No one is perfect. At forty-two years of age, I am finally choosing not to set this trap for myself or others. I didn't have the tools to spring the trap back then. I got caught, and I got hurt. So did others.

Robert battled his own windmills. His childhood had left his heart full of holes he was hoping to fill. We made the mistake of trying to use each other to fill the voids in our lives. Two broken people coming together do not unite and become whole. Only two whole people can come together to be one.

I thought if I ignored my needs and worked hard to fill Robert's needs, he would be happy and, therefore, I would be happy. Little by little, I repressed parts of my personality, hoping to avoid conflict. Several of my friends felt I was pulling away and commented on it. My mother said I wasn't myself anymore. I thought so little of myself at the time, it mattered not. If I gained his love, it was worth losing myself.

We decided to marry that summer. By then, my father had left my mother. I refused to allow him to walk me down the aisle. A kind professor we called Dr. Pat agreed to stand in. I will never forget him.

We were married in the Catholic student chapel. Robert's parents refused to come to the wedding. A Catholic wedding was regarded as an insult due to their estranged relationship with his birth father. I agreed to a non-denominational wedding; however, my mother refused to come unless it was Catholic. After wrestling with the decision, Robert and I decided to go through with our original plans. It was a small, modest Catholic wedding with a few close friends. My mother did attend, and his parents did not. I believe Robert always regretted the choice and blamed me for the hurt it caused his mother.

I felt like a failure from the wedding night to the day we divorced. I never felt good enough for Robert. At times, I tried too hard; other times, I gave up and buried myself in graduate school and then in my teaching job. It was not long before Robert lost interest.

There were signs that there was another woman; however, I chose to live under a veil of denial. Finally, the veil dropped, and I could no longer deny the truth. Robert had been seeing another woman. A close friend told me he did not believe she was the first.

My initial feelings were of hopelessness, helplessness and worthlessness. I felt like discarded garbage. Teaching my first-grade class was my only lifeline.

I requested we try counseling as a desperate last straw, and he agreed. We went several times together and separately. I don't remember the name of the counselor, but I remember the way he looked as he leaned forward on his desk and asked me, "Do you really want someone who does not love you?"

I felt I was once again defeated. Robert moved out, and I needed a roommate to help with expenses.

I can't remember the details of how you and I ended up together, Becky. I can only remember feeling shocked that you would consider living with me. You were so beautiful and sophisticated, and I was such a plain Jane.

I still have a faded copy of the diet you and I went on that first summer. I lost so much weight, I convinced half the faculty to join us. Remember the charts and stars I made for the faculty lunchroom?

You encouraged me to break the Laura Ingalls Wilder mold and update my wardrobe. It wasn't long before you introduced me to the world of credit cards. Your motto was, "If you like it, buy it." I can still feel that sinking feeling in my stomach when I received a bank notice stating that I had bounced a check. You had assured me the check would not go through before we deposited our paychecks on Friday. I learned you were not always right, but you were always sincere. Becky, you were a true friend, and I believe with all my heart that you were God-sent. Living with you taught me how to laugh again.

I will never forget our bus trip to Jacksonville. We were going to get a physical and take tests for the Air Force. Your mother had told us the Air Force would be a great way for two young women to see the world. I was ready, and I persuaded you to go. The recruiter in Tampa loved us, and he enthusiastically made all the arrangements.

We were to take a late-night bus. I told you I was afraid to ride the bus at night, and we needed to dress like nuns for protection. Somehow, I got you to agree, but trying to dress you down was a difficult task. I finally persuaded you to wear my gray jumper with a white blouse. I had an official nun's veil for my head, but we had to settle for a white pillowcase from my dorm days for you. I kept trying to tuck the part stamped "National Linen Company" under. To help create the illusion, you agreed to wear my old wire-rimmed glasses. The lenses had been taken out long before. There was no way I could persuade you to go without make-up. Your eyelashes were made to wear mascara. However, when you reached through the empty glasses frames to rub your eye, I thought the old woman in the bus station was about to drop her teeth. On the bus, we held up Bibles in front of our faces as we laughed at people's reactions. I am so grateful God is full of mercy and forgiveness. You and I deserved much less.

When we got to Jacksonville, a kind police officer offered to drive us to the AFEES. (I still don't know what those letters stand for. Thank heavens he knew where it was.) Your Presbyterian background had not prepared you for the officer's inquiries to two nuns; however, I must say I handled it like a pro. I told him we were part of an experimental project hoping to get the Catholic Church more involved in the real world. We were going to be teachers at the Air Force bases. The tale I was weaving was so full of holes it is a miracle we weren't hauled in for questioning. You were as nervous as a cat. You kept hitting my leg with your foot. I had to keep talking to prevent bursting into laughter.

When we finally arrived, it occurred to us that we would be surrounded by single men. Before we went to check in, we whipped off the nun veils. Even in our drab gray garb, we attracted whistles and catcalls. At first, it was flattering, but by the time we got to our room, we were scared to death. The phone rang all night with invitations to sell our souls. When the guys started banging on the door, you locked yourself in the bathroom. It finally occurred to us to call the front desk, and security officers came to remove our visitors.

The next day, we were to be downstairs at 5 A.M., but we were late and missed the bus. It was my fault. My hair took forever to blow dry. You were a little annoyed, but the Air Force sent over a special driver. Because we were potential officer candidates, we received preferential treatment until the physical. I can't believe we endured those examinations. I can't even bring myself to write the details. Remembering is enough.

The crowning blow was the written tests. I have always been a poor test-taker, but I was without a clue as to how to answer the questions. I guessed at half and just made dot designs filling in the other half. You, on the other hand, resorted to dishonesty and copied off the guy in front of you. After we made it home, which was a miracle in itself, I called the recruiter for my test scores. I thought I had heard him wrong when he said, "10 and 10." I said, "Ten! Out of one hundred?" When I asked your scores, he told me you had done a little better. I was jealous because I knew you had cheated; however, it didn't get you far. Your scores were 15 and 20. I can't believe they were willing to take us as officers. We told stories about the AFEES for weeks in the teachers' lunchroom.

You and I began to develop quite a reputation as "The Dynamic Duo." We were devoted teachers during the week and devoted partiers on the weekend. We had no shame as we flirted with men at T.G.I. Fridays, got them to buy us dinner, excused ourselves to the rest room and left to go home. We bought Snickers bars and doughnuts and laughed all night. I laughed a lot, but I wasn't really happy. All the laughter was only a camouflage covering my pain.

Deep down, I still felt like a failure because of my broken marriage. Robert began to reel me back and forth like a yo-yo as he experienced ups and downs with the other woman. Each time I agreed to try again, it ended in the familiar pattern of rejection. I was finally the one who applied for the divorce. You were such a true friend to go to court with me the day the divorce was granted. It was amazing how quickly the proceedings were finalized. In less than half an hour, all my dreams were dissolved.

The next week, I made an appointment with a priest to begin annulment proceedings. I could not imagine my life without a seal of approval from the Catholic Church. The priest was cold and harsh. The paperwork was endless. The questions on the pages demanded to know every humiliating detail. My parents, Robert's parents and Robert were also requested to participate. My parents had recently reunited; I did not want to burden them with the details of my broken marriage as they struggled to repair their own. Robert refused to cooperate. He said he might one day pursue a political career, and he wanted no public record of adultery. I did not even consider asking his parents for help. Even if they had any feelings for me, they could not overcome their bitterness toward the Catholic Church.

Although I tried to deny it, feelings of bitterness were beginning to contaminate my Catholic whitewash. You and I were both thirsty for something besides the beer we were drinking on the weekends to convince us we were happy. The friendship and the fun were only bandages covering the need for healing. It is by grace alone that the dirtiest waters of my past led me to the spring of everlasting life.

Both of us were fond of a second-grade teacher named Linda, one of the funniest people we knew. She had blunt opinions and expressed them in a colorful way. Many times, she said things people were thinking but would never dare to say. Yet, there was a sincerity and a commitment to something. She was always talking about some project she was involved with at her Baptist church. When I asked her why that church made her so happy, she said, "Come and see."

When I visited her church, you went with me. By this point in our lives, you and I rarely went anywhere without each other. My favorite times were visiting your parents in Tarpon Springs. They treated me like royalty, yet, at the same time, they made me feel like a member of the family. You and I became members of another family a month after our first visit to Spencer Baptist Church: the family of believers. Once again, we were treated like royalty. We became children of the King.

I know God has special plans for our lives, Becky. We were at a point in our lives when the temptations to make poor choices were becoming greater and greater. In the eyes of the world, we did nothing to bring us great shame, but as we entered the presence of a pure, holy God, we became grateful for a Savior who washes our sins away.

Just at the time Jesus came into my heart, Rob Smith came into my life. He was one of many blind dates. He was obviously God's choice for my life mate. I was married a year later, and you were my maid of honor. The following year, you married, and I was honored to be your matron of honor.

We have shared the most important days of our lives together: the day we became Christians and our wedding days. I can't think of anyone I would have rather shared them with.

I praise the God who brought us together as friends and who brought us to His Son, Jesus Christ. It was all part of a plan, lovingly designed for both of our lives. I feel a closeness to you that will remain a part of me forever.

You will always be special to me. I love you, Becky.

XV

Rob

Dear Rob,

Recently, we celebrated our sixteenth wedding anniversary. In three days, you will be forty-three years old. How blessed I feel to have been chosen to spend all these years with you. Without a doubt, it was part of God's perfect plan for my life, and I am thankful.

I know exactly how you looked the first time I saw you. I still have the shirt you were wearing. Even though years later, you tossed it in a pile of clothes to be given to charity, I put it aside. It hangs in the back of my closet, ever reminding me of the tall, thin prince who rode into my life—even if you did not come in a Porsche, as I had been led to believe.

Having suffered a painful divorce, I found myself on the caseload of many of my matchmaker friends. I was matched with every brother, uncle and next-door neighbor the faculty of Quail Hollow Elementary School could find. Even one of my first-graders tried to fix me up with her widowed father.

I tried them all. Of course, by date time, my opinions were already biased after Becky gave me her prior evaluation of each one as she examined them through the kitchen window of our apartment. I had just about given up after the ex-priest. He came dressed in a yellow rain slicker. Seeing his skinny legs, glasses and huge nose, Becky informed me, "Big Bird has arrived." After that evening of hiding behind a menu and hoping no one would see me, I was about to call it quits. You know the rest. While explaining to a mutual friend that I needed a spark, I spotted your picture in her wedding album. "Someone like this is what I had in mind," I said. Her husband explained that you and he had been childhood friends. He told me you were an engineer who drove a Porsche, and he promised he would call you. That sounded pretty good to a divorced first-grade teacher who had just been out with Big Bird.

Four months later, you agreed to the date. You insist it was an aerospace project that delayed your response. I still think you were getting up your nerve to go out with a divorced ex-nun.

Traveling from Orlando to Tampa for our date, you were two (or was it three?) hours late. Instead of the midnight blue Porsche I was told you drove, you came in a vanilla-colored Mercury Cougar. You had just sold your Porsche and given up your job as an engineer to go back to school for a Ph.D.

I begged Becky to stay in her room. I was afraid that if you saw her first, you would never want to go out with me. She refused and proceeded to describe you as she peered from our kitchen window. "Bell Bottom Blues," she called you. Well, it was better than "Big Bird."

You were polite and kind. There was a definite chemistry between us, although, in the back of my mind, I wondered if you might be a bit boring for me. You passed the test when you agreed to fly paper airplanes from the roof of the Tampa airport. It sounds like something right out of a Gidget movie. I'm a little embarrassed I even suggested it.

That night when you brought me home, I invited you in to talk. You had told me earlier that evening that you were a Southern Baptist. My commitment to the Catholic Church was wavering as I wrestled with the mounds of intrusive paperwork required for an annulment. I enjoyed the visits I had been making with Becky to the Baptist church. It was a refreshing change of pace. I just couldn't understand the part at the end when the preacher gave an invitation to anyone wanting to "be saved." I thought only TV preachers said that kind of stuff. Besides, I had spent two years in a convent. I surely had covered my bases—hadn't I?

I asked you question after question, and you pointed me back to the same scriptures my friend had shown me, the same thing I heard the preacher say. Part of me wondered if all the Baptists in the world spoke in codes. I know now that the Word of God is not a secret code—it is life itself.

How grateful I am that God had brought me to a point where I was ready to listen. The Lord used you to speak to me that night. We talked until four o'clock in the morning. As we said good-night, I waited as patiently as I could while you politely fumbled around. Finally, I could not stand it any longer. About to explode with the awkward formalities, I blurted out, "Are you going to kiss me or not?" You should have known from that moment what you were getting into!

During that week, I reviewed the scriptures you had given me. I wondered why I had never heard God's plan for my salvation so clearly until then. I know I believed that Jesus was the Son of God and that He died for me. However, I never had that assurance that I was going to heaven. I figured I had a 50/50 chance, depending on the sins of that day. How freeing it is to know that the price was paid at the cross! My admission ticket is grace, not my works. "For it is by grace you have been saved, through faith—and this not from yourselves, it is the gift of God—not by works, so that no one can boast" (Eph. 2:8–9).

I shared every thought with Becky. She had become like a sister to me. When we went to church that next

Sunday, I felt her nudging me at the invitation. Both of us walked the aisle that Sunday. Blessed assurance, Jesus was ours.

The following Sunday, we were baptized. It meant so much to me that you made a special trip to be there for me.

I was so excited that day. I felt God had been drawing me near, and I was sure you were part of His plan for my life. Yet I struggled with the stigma of being a divorced woman. The person assigned to counsel me on my decision to accept Jesus as my Savior felt she needed to tell me her views on divorce. The woman explained that if I married you, I would be committing adultery and leading you to do the same. I felt condemned and confused. I cried for hours on a day that was supposed to be the happiest day of my life.

I have forgiven that woman, but I do feel she was wrong. It was not her place to judge my situation, especially on the day I was greeting my Savior into my heart. I did make an appointment with the preacher for that week. He showed me the words in 1 Corinthians 7:15:

> But if the unbeliever leaves, let him do so. A believing man or woman is not bound in such circumstances; God has called us to live in peace.

That verse brought me the peace I was seeking. I regret the years I was out of God's will and the choices I made that led to my consequences. I am grateful for the Redeemer who washed my sins away.

You always made me feel brand-new. However, the temptation to feel "secondhand" continually loomed over me. You always made me feel cherished, yet at first, my low self-esteem prevented me from accepting your love completely. Your kindness was a bit overwhelming. I began to play hide-and-seek. After a series of unanswered phone messages, you confronted me. When I realized there was a possibility of losing you, I made a choice. I allowed myself to fall in love with you. It was one of the best decisions of my life.

We were married the next year. We had a beautiful, simple wedding at Spencer Memorial Baptist Church, where I had made my profession of faith. Becky was the maid of honor, and your sisters were my bridesmaids. My mother and my Sunday school teacher decorated the church hall for the reception. The mothers of my Brownie Scout troop made the wedding cake and the punch as a gift. Two children from my first-grade class served as the flower girl and ring bearer. I was surrounded by friends and family. It was a real wedding, a new beginning for me.

It was significant that my father walked me down the aisle. I had forgiven him for his unfaithfulness to my mother. I felt God had given me a brand-new start; all my past had been forgiven. I needed to allow my father to experience that same grace. I was able to forgive because I had been forgiven.

Shortly after we were married, I received a phone call that Robert, my ex-husband, had been killed in a car accident. I battled with feelings of guilt and remorse because my initial response was one of relief. The words of the woman at the church had been haunting me like a ghost. Even on the day we married, I feared I was leading you into sin because I was divorced. When Robert died, I finally felt free of that fear. I can hardly believe I have the nerve to write those words. For so long, I was ashamed of those feelings. I never really dealt with Robert's death. I didn't know how to grieve. I wasn't his widow—who was I? I had chosen to block out my entire relationship with him as if it had never happened. I have learned the hard way that pretending does not make anything go away. The unresolved pain from my first marriage created a trust vacuum in our relationship. I loved you, but part of me was determined never to allow myself to be totally vulnerable.

Eight years later, when we went on a marriage retreat, I finally dealt with those injured feelings. You had been paying the price for those hurts as I withheld part of my inner self from you. As I poured out those feelings of hurt and betrayal, I will always remember the way you responded. You explained that you always knew you loved me more than I loved you, but it didn't matter. The love I was able to give you was enough. Since that day, I have been able to give you more and more. Once I acknowledged my pain and brought it into the open, I have allowed it to heal. I have made peace with my past. My prayer is that Robert accepted Jesus as his Savior before he died.

I thank God for the way He has used my divorce to allow me to empathize with others in similar circumstances. Although my divorce was not as traumatic and complicated as most, I still experienced enough brokenness to feel compassion for people suffering through the process. I pray they will find mates who will make them as happy as you have made me.

All of our married life has been divided into four-year segments as we completed your education. Four years in Tallahassee to complete your Ph.D., four years in Atlanta for medical school and four years in St. Louis for residency. We are finally breaking the pattern, as we begin our fifth year in Pensacola, now that you are a practicing radiologist.

The first four years were the hardest. I am grateful that your sister Julie lived with us for the first month. Soon, I learned you were not perfect. You are quick to blow up and quick to calm down. She could handle you like a pro. It has taken years for me to get the hang of it. My method is to hold on, suffer loudly while I analyze, and then talk it to death. After sixteen years, we are much closer to a healthy balance.

You have always tried to make me happy, Rob. At times, I know I've frustrated you because I seemed to choose feeling miserable, no matter how hard you tried. You did not have the key to my happiness. I had the key, but for so long, I was afraid to use it. My feelings of insecurity deceived me into believing I was not good enough to deserve true happiness.

During the first four years of our marriage, I made myself a prisoner in my own home. Being a teacher in a legalistic Christian school did not help. How sad it is the way organized religion can kill grace. You had tried to tell me that I would not be happy teaching in that school. It was not the first (or the last) time I didn't listen. I was a new Christian and was naïve enough to believe all Christians were kind, wonderful people. I hadn't grown to realize Christians are sinners saved by grace, and many times, that sin nature wins the battle. It is especially sad when legalism wins over grace. It is killing our churches. Part of my spirit was killed that year. How relieved I felt when my contract ended and we were free to join another church in Tallahassee.

I have warm memories about every church we've joined since then. Our church families have become my extended family. There are so many people who have touched my life and made a difference.

I didn't have many friends in Tallahassee. I was afraid to drive, especially after Robert died. I was always afraid that I would have an accident and kill Lindsey. My fear of car accidents overwhelmed me. Do you remember how many times I called the hospital and the police when you were late? You were always back in the cold room in the lab, and you couldn't hear the phone. I was picturing you in a morgue. It's funny now, but it wasn't funny at the time. My fears consumed me. I think I always felt I didn't deserve you, and one day, you would be taken away. I just couldn't take hold of that key that would unlock the door to set me free from the dungeon of insecurity.

I resisted using that key all through the second four-year chapter of our lives. Once again, we had a church family who brought light through the keyhole. Clairmont Hills Baptist Church in Atlanta was truly a ray of light. We lived in seven hundred square feet of student housing. We were supported by scholarships, your consulting jobs and loans. Gifts from your parents and mine were like manna in the desert. Twenty dollars a month from your granny was a luxury, and my tutoring money paid for diapers. Coupons were a way of life. Financially, we had nothing to offer our church. We could not tithe borrowed money, yet never have I felt more like an heir to the King. Under the humble leadership of Larry Burgess, supported by his wife, Nancy, Clairmont Hills was the lifeboat that kept us afloat during the topsy-turvy days of medical school.

We weathered the storm. I even gave birth to our son during that time. Unlike Lindsey, he was in the church nursery within a month. Edna Robinson, his personal guardian angel, had prepared his place in the nursery months before he arrived. It was easy to release him into her waiting arms of love.

If church was my haven, our home continued to be my self-made prison. While you were disciplining your mind at medical school, I struggled with how to discipline our strong-willed daughter and nurture our newborn son. I felt inadequate and unprepared for mothering. No matter what I did, I felt it was a mistake. I rejected suggestions from family as criticism.

Our neighbors served as a network of support. We had a black seminary student and his family on the right and Mormon dental students on the left. My favorite was the Chinese lady who wanted to learn how to bake a cake from a cake mix. In exchange for sharing my cooking expertise, we feasted on many Oriental treats. God's love comes in many flavors.

Although it was a hard four years for both of us, I have never been more proud than I was on the day of your graduation. All of a sudden, all the struggles seemed worth the prize. I felt our lives had been a scene out of "St. Elsewhere," but graduation gave that chapter a happy ending.

Your parents bought us a Chevy Cavalier as a congratulatory gift. It was a welcome sight because our old car would never have made that long road to St. Louis. Of course, the trip had its problems. The car was loaded with your precious albums because you were afraid they would get too hot in the moving van. Records were stacked in every available space. Our children were separated by a wall of albums. Every time you turned a corner, a stack fell on Bobby's head. He cried, I screamed, Lindsey complained, and you looked straight ahead, saying nothing. We alternated between Sesame Street tapes and stories from Teddy Ruxpin. After many hours, your voice sounded like thunder. Teddy would be thrown out the window if he said one more simple word to "Grubby." The thought of Teddy Ruxpin as a highway casualty was just enough to send our children over the edge. Cries of utter trauma filled our car.

The only thing that could add the crowning touch to all that stress would be a flat tire. Changing the tire in

102-degree heat was your penance for making us ride with all those albums. After eighteen hours, we entered St. Louis. Seeing the statues of the Blessed Virgin that graced many front lawns, I wondered if I would have been better off if I had stayed in the convent!

St. Louis will always mark a significant chapter in my life. The pages of those four years will be folded at the corners forever. During the time we spent there as you completed your residency, I was finally able to use the key that had kept me locked within my own walls. I will never forget the outpouring of love I experienced as the Lord unlocked the door in the imprisoning walls built by the unhappiness of my childhood.

We have it all, Rob. I guess the greatest truth I discovered when I used that magical key was that we've had it all along.

Thank you for waiting for my heart to be set free.

XVI

Bobby

My dear son,

Just a week ago, you celebrated your eleventh birthday. It is a joy and privilege to watch you grow and enjoy your life so fully. You were part of our lives long before the day of your birth. We had prayed for you, and God had prepared a place for you in our hearts. The Bible says God knew you before you were born, and even when you were just a tiny baby inside of me, He was knitting you together. Every part of you has been marvelously made.

I am so grateful to be your mommy. When it was time for you to arrive, my body wouldn't cooperate, and the drugs used to help me along were too harsh for your little heart. I was afraid I would lose you. I had known for months that you were a boy. Daddy and I wanted a little boy, and we were so happy. In a way, I was afraid to be that happy. That is what the devil does, my son. He tries to trick us into being fearful and expecting God to let us down. I pray with all my heart that you will grow to be a man strong in your faith, able to shield yourself from the devil's arrows of doubt and fear. I've asked God to make me into the mother you need to guide you as you grow. I believe God has heard my prayer and will be faithful to answer. He began a good work in each of us, and He promises to complete it.

I wish I had been further along in the process when you were a little boy. In some ways, when I look back, it seems you and Lindsey were being raised by a scared little girl. My life was haunted with fears. The biggest one was the fear of failure. I wanted badly to be a good mother for both of you, but I didn't know how.

Lindsey was a challenging little girl. She was always three steps ahead of me. As I struggled to keep up with her, you waited patiently on the back burner. You were an easy, quiet baby. It's almost as if you knew I needed someone to love with no demands. You were so easy to love. You cuddled and smiled and told me you "yuvved" me almost as soon as you could speak. Everyone adored you the minute they met you.

I put you in a mother's-morning-out program one day a week when you were two years old. All the mothers told me your playmates went home chattering "Bobby" from one week to the next.

You were able to charm everyone except your sister, Lindsey. Perhaps it was hard for her to deal with a little brother who attracted others so effortlessly. Perhaps it was because, although I have described you as a perfect angel, you were also a normal little boy, prone to running into Lindsey's room uninvited, knocking down all her carefully placed My Little Ponies and running out of the room with a smile. You left her screaming in frustration.

It has always been hard to discipline you because you are so repentant and crushed when you fail to please. For a long time, it was hard to believe you were ever at fault because you had mastered that sweet, innocent look. After eleven years, I've finally caught on, with a lot of unsolicited help from your sister.

We moved to St. Louis when you were two, almost three. You and I were both granted a reprieve from our apartment life when you began preschool. It was like a rebirth for me. Once again, I was allowed to return to one of my greatest passions—teaching. Teaching was the one thing I felt I could do and do right. As hard as I tried to be a good mommy, I had the feeling I was always doing it wrong. Having twelve precious preschool children who loved "Miss Michelle" helped to quiet the monster inside of my head, telling me I wasn't good enough to be loved. Bobby, in many ways, you and I are very much alike. I work hard for people to like me the way you work for a sticker on a paper. The difference is that you like yourself, and the sticker is for what you have done. Mommy didn't like herself. I wanted the approval of others, so I tried to fill up all the places where I felt I didn't measure up. This is hard to explain to one so young, but one day, I feel you will understand. You have been blessed with a tender heart.

It was your sensitivity that finally broke through the fragile mask I wore for so long. Telling this story still breaks my heart. The incident happened on the day for hearts, Valentine's Day. Holidays in preschool classes are an extra-special time. I had been up late the night before, cutting out paper hearts for my preschoolers. I couldn't wait to get to school that day. I was dressed in my red jumper, the one I saved to wear especially on Christmas and Valentine's Day. When it was time to go, I called up the stairs for you to come. When you didn't come, I called again...and again. By the third time, my voice had reached a new pitch. When you finally came, you hadn't combed your hair or brushed your teeth. I was so angry. I screamed my loudest and ordered you to go back, comb that hair, and brush those teeth. You could not move quickly enough to please me. I continued to scream. I still see your little face. You were so scared of me as you rushed in, trying desperately to satisfy the crazy monster I had become. When we finally got in the car, I asked you if you had turned off the television. You were afraid to admit to me that you had not. I jerked the car door open and slammed it shut just as I had the front door.

I screamed all the way to school. You cried and shook and tried to apologize. I told you to shut up.

I don't know what kind of a day you had that day. I thank God for people like your teachers, Miss Alice and Miss Ellen, who love little children with or without combed hair or brushed teeth. Somehow, the little hearts I had cut out and the lesson I had planned on "Jesus loves you" did not feel right that day. I no longer felt pretty in my red jumper. I felt ugly. The mean red monster had finally come out. Do you know what a hypocrite is, Bobby? It is a person who says one thing and does another. I was a hypocrite: I told the children Jesus loved them, and I missed the chance to show that kind of love to you.

I don't even know if you remember all of this, but I will never forget it. I have asked God many times to forgive me. I believe He did the first time I asked. My guilt and shame made me ask again and again. I want you to know that I'm truly sorry. You were just a little boy. Nothing you did deserved the screaming tirade that you received.

That afternoon, a mother of one of my students called to compliment me on my teaching. After my actions, there was no way I could accept her praise, so I confided in her about the events of our morning. I hoped she would tell me that all mothers acted like that sometimes. Instead, she surprised me by suggesting I might have a hidden reason for being angry. She explained that her father was an alcoholic, and growing up for her had been a stressful, confusing time. As a child, she was never able to express her fear or anger. It amazed me that she seemed to be able to see right through me. The episode I had described reminded her of herself before she began attending a group called Adult Children of Alcoholics. She suggested that maybe I had a similar problem and would like to come.

I wasn't sure if a group like that could help me. Besides, you know how unpredictable Daddy's schedule can be. I never guessed he would be home in time for me to go. Not only was he on time, but he encouraged me to go. I continued to go every Tuesday night for the next year and a half. During that time, I began to remember some sad things about my life as a little girl, and I started to see a counselor. At first, the things I remembered were too hard to talk about, but I wrote long letters to my counselor. Then I would talk it all out with Miss Gwen. Do you remember how you loved your little friend, Grant? His mother, Miss Gwen, was like an angel to me. While you were playing with Grant, she was listening to me. She made me coffee and served it in clear glass cups painted with little white ducks. Each cup of coffee was like a cup of cold water in a dry desert. She did not fully understand my pain; however, she was a compassionate listener. I will never forget her.

I will also never forget your Daddy's strong arms during that time. My prayer for you is that you will grow to have the strength of character Daddy has. At my weakest point, he was my strength. He was doing his residency at that time and working long, hard hours. Many nights, he found me sitting in a corner of our bedroom crying and rubbing my arms. He held me and comforted me and made me believe I could make it through one more day. I did my best to keep you and Lindsey from seeing me cry.

I made it through, one day at a time. At one point, I stopped being so sad and became angry. It seemed unfair that my childhood had been that unhappy. Sometimes, when we are angry about something deep inside, we show it on the outside about some insignificant thing. That is why it is important to take care of the inside hurts; otherwise, the pain inside causes us to strike out and hurt others. I did hurt a dear friend of mine during this stormy time. You will be surprised to know it was Miss Kim.

A conflict came up between the weekday preschool and the Sunday school. What was a trivial territorial issue became a war for me. I was ready to fight and determined to win. No one had ever seen this side of my personality. It had always been there, but it had been buried for years. I had never dealt with my past anger, and I was ready to fight every battle right then and there on the preschool playground.

I soon found that no one was fighting but me. I am embarrassed when I remember my actions. I am grateful to Miss Kim for refusing to fight back. She just loved me through it. As you know, she is now one of my closest friends.

As time went on, I became less angry. I was able to stop seeing the counselor. About this time, I stopped going to my ACA group. You see, I was depending heavily on Jesus during my sad times because I saw that He was the only way out of my dark past, yet I was not allowed to mention His precious name in the meetings. So I felt that I had received all that such a group could offer.

God knew I would need someone to help and support me during this time. I feel He placed me in the tender hands of one of His most faithful servants, Miss Pam. She became like a mother to me. She took me under her wing and taught me so much about my heavenly Father. Because of her guidance, I learned many spiritual truths. I learned I am a child of the King, Bobby, and so are you.

I am so proud to be your mother. You are a light

unashamed to shine, a city on a hill. I pray you will always let Jesus use your personality to glorify Him. He has given you your sense of humor, your keen mind, your artistic talent and your tender heart. I thank God for you, my dear little boy.

I love you so much that hurting you broke my heart. I thank God that the result of this painful incident was that I overcame the monster. I was able to face the evil one who deceived me into believing I could never love without fear. The victory was in Jesus, who said Greater is he who is in [me], than he who is in the world (1 John 4:4, NAS). I was broken in the battle, but by the grace of God, He put me back together, and with His help, I will try to be the mother you need and deserve.

I am excited about all that God has in store for you, my son. The future looks bright. Learn from my past. "All things work together for good to those who love God" (Rom. 8:28, NKJV). Love God first. Make friends who will listen, forgive and lead you close to Jesus. Become a man with strong arms and wide shoulders like your Daddy. And always know I love you.

XVII

Joyce

Dear Joyce,

The first time I saw you was at my front door in Pensacola. You and two of your sweet children were standing there smiling. I thought, *All those people have the same face, just on different bodies.* You were all so cute. I, on the other hand, looked terrible. My eyes were puffy from crying. I had no makeup, and my hair was pulled back in a stringy ponytail. All the shades were drawn, and the house was dark. The only light came from the television playing a videotape of my good-bye party from my church in St. Louis. It was about the thirty-eighth time I had watched the tape. I wept every time, always building to a crescendo of wails when the song "Friends Are Friends Forever" was sung at the end. I made you watch part of it with me as I tearfully told you about everyone on the tape. You later told me you left my house that day thinking I would be too depressing to have for a friend.

I kept up that routine for three straight weeks. Finally, school started, and I was forced out of my house to drive my children to school. The drive was along Pensacola Bay. As I watched the sun glistening on the water and realized I was finally living in a real house, surrounded by kind neighbors, I thought maybe I would stop crying and start trying to adjust. My life was not too tough. I could finally buy groceries without a handful of coupons.

I eventually began to respond to new acquaintances. I remember admiring your long, brown hair falling neatly over your shoulders and down your back. I've been letting my hair grow ever since, but somehow, it doesn't look like yours. If it gets any longer, I will look like a wilted country-western singer. You never look wilted, although you try hard to be a wallflower. Refusing to accept any attention for yourself, you always encourage others to bask in their spotlights. You are usually the one "working the lights." It is evident that you know the Source of power, and He has gifted you with the ability to allow others to shine.

I shine best surrounded by a body of believers, and finding a new church home was my greatest priority. It was important for me to find my place in the center of God's will. I researched the local churches the way high-schoolers look at colleges. You became my sounding board as I evaluated each one. The biggest problem was that there were so many good choices.

The last place I imagined myself was First Baptist Church. I assumed it was filled with rich snobs and pharisees. I am so happy my assumptions were incorrect. It was one of the friendliest churches I visited. Our family was welcomed with open arms. Although I was accustomed to a more contemporary church setting, I have come to appreciate the traditional and conservative atmosphere.

After four years, I feel I've carved out my niche at First Baptist Church. There wasn't a place for someone like me who colors outside the lines. I had to create my own place. Dressing up in a black mouse suit to tell children about Jesus is the closest thing I could get to wearing a nun habit in a Baptist church, I suppose. You shared every idea in the birth of Minute Mouse, the church mouse, listening to me rehearse and watching me perform. You are always there behind the scenes. Without your encouragement, I know Minute Mouse never would have gone to Russia with the choir mission trip. I was ready to give it up because I felt my motives were wrong. You told me matter of factly that if my motives were wrong, I should change my motives, not give up the trip. The trip changed my motives and my life. I realized how blessed I am to live in a nation that always has allowed me to worship my Lord and Savior openly. I will never forget the small-statured Russian women standing for hours on callous feet in non-air-conditioned churches, their scarfed heads bowed in reverent thankfulness for the opportunity to hear God's Word openly proclaimed in a church setting. I'm so glad I went. Thank you for encouraging me.

You also encouraged my greatest performance on my fortieth birthday. Sixteen of my dearest St. Louis friends were joined in a local restaurant by eight of my Pensacola friends who I thought could handle the "real" me. I sang "What a Difference You Made in My Life" into a salt shaker. Amy Grant sang back-up on a nearby cassette player. My St. Louis friends dressed like nuns and sang to me songs from *Sister Act.* My new Pensacola friends sang an original tune titled "You Are My Honey" (to the tune of "You Are My Sunshine"). Other people in the restaurant kept asking what we were drinking. The shocked waiter kept saying, "Iced tea—they're Baptists!" It was one of the happiest days of my life.

Unlike most normal people, another one of my happiest days was when I went into the hospital to have a hysterectomy. I had all new pink and white nightgowns and a plastic name band around my wrist. I told everyone about my surgery weeks in advance and suggested that balloons were preferred over flowers. I had even packed Scotch tape for my many cards and posters.

You came bearing a plant the morning of my surgery. No one could inflate helium balloons that early, you apologized. It didn't matter. I was just happy to see you. You always make me feel like I'm amusing because you laugh at everything I say. I made a crack about filling the plastic bedpan with candy for the nurses. While I was in surgery, you bought the candy. It became quite a conversation piece, exactly what I desired.

I couldn't believe you stayed the entire time I was in surgery. Although my vision was like a quick-rolling filmstrip, when I opened my eyes, I recognized your cute face. I will always remember that you were there for me.

My fantasy of a balloon-filled, attention-seeking adventure came true. I recovered well from surgery and sat up in bed like a princess on a throne. When I wasn't entertaining guests, I was knitting slippers for the nurses. I felt popular. You were there often, laughing in amazement that anyone would gain so much pleasure from a hysterectomy.

The dream quickly became a nightmare, however, when I developed some serious problems. For the next four days, I was unable to hold anything in my stomach. I unplugged my phone and had a "No visitors" sign posted on my door. The princess was not welcoming anyone into her court. I spent most of my time in the bathroom. The nurses were still enjoying the candy from the bedpan, but they did not enjoy seeking new veins in my arms and legs to stick with IV needles. I was so weak I thought I would die. If I couldn't die, at least I wanted to go home. I had had enough of the hospital, but I was told I couldn't leave until I could hold down some food. I couldn't even hold down water.

I was so happy when I went home. I lied and said I held down some green Jell-O just to get out of there. The first thing I held down was the homemade soup you brought for me. You filled a pot big enough to feed an army. I laughed at first, but it became the only thing I could eat for days. My friends brought meals and more meals (just as I had requested), and each came with a rich dessert (also by request). Many had to be frozen to enjoy later. The only thing I could handle was the soup. You provided exactly what I needed.

Joyce, only a God who loves me very much could have known I would need a humble, selfless friend with a true servant's heart to balance my attention-seeking personality. The thing I cherish most is that you are able to look deeply and see past my ego and recognize the heart that desires to love the Lord with my entire being. I have learned more about mothering from you than from a hundred parenting manuals. You know how to balance practicality and humor.

I believe with all my heart that God prepared a place for me in Pensacola long before I arrived. He knew I would need a neighbor and a friend just like you.

XVIII

Pop Pop

Dear Pop Pop,

Not long ago, I attended the funeral of the father-in-law of one of my husband's friends.

I never knew him, but he was obviously a kind, generous man, and he left his family a legacy of loving memories. I know he will be missed greatly, especially by his oldest grandson, Mark. He was the one most freely shedding the tears everyone else was carrying in their heavy hearts. As I watched his broad shoulders shake, I could hear his quiet sobs. A close family friend removed his glasses for him as they were beginning to fill with tears and drip.

I felt I was watching the entire scene through Mark's glasses. My own vision was blurred as I remembered how much I loved you and miss you.

I grieved about not writing to you the last years of your life. You waited patiently for my letters and even sent books of stamps to encourage me. There is no stamp that will take this letter to you now. You are gone, and I grieve for you with the same pain I saw in Mark's eyes. This was the first time I have faced these feelings. When you died, my method of dealing with pain was to stuff and deny. I did not get to go to your funeral. You died shortly after my divorce, and I did not have the money to fly to Maryland. As I look back now, I admit I used that as an excuse. Not going to the funeral was a way to avoid the pain. In many ways, I just blocked you out.

I can see now that I have been trying to "get you back" as I've developed close relationships with several senior pastors. My heart is easily drawn to silver-haired men who blend wisdom with humor and strive only to bring people to Jesus. That is what you did, Pop Pop.

You had a great influence on my life. I remember that when I told Nana I was going to be a nun, she told me it was "in the genes." She said I had inherited my call to the ministry from you. At the time you felt called to preach, it was not feasible to pursue seminary training. The Depression was in full swing, and your job at the B&O Railroad barely covered the expenses of your wife and young children. Hungry to learn, you studied diligently with a mentor in the evenings. The shelves in your basement were quickly filled with spiritual books. They filled your mind and heart until you found the place God had planned for the glorious overflow.

Every Tuesday night, you went into the deepest, darkest boweries of Baltimore, where you preached to drunks and hoboes. I remember reading a newspaper article that described the way you attracted a crowd by bending pennies in your bare hands. Once you had their attention, you told them about the true source of your strength, Jesus Christ.

Your hands were huge and strong. I remember how secure I felt when you held my hand during our long walks to the drugstore. I think of you whenever I see a picture of the Praying Hands because you are the one who taught me how to pray.

Unlike Nana, I don't think my early call to ministry was inherited. I believe it came to me by way of example. You were my greatest role model of a true Christian. The memory of your praying hands, faithful even when wracked with arthritis, helps me to realize the hand of God has always been upon me.

I know that you prayed for me from the day I was born until the day you died. Although there have been times when I have feared you were watching me from heaven with disappointment, I believe now that you see me with eyes of grace. Hopefully, you see that my heart's desire is to be an empty vessel, longing to be filled with Jesus.

You used to quote to me one of your favorite hymns:

> Have thine own way, Lord.
> Have thine own way.
> Thou art the potter;
> I am the clay.

At one time, my will was as hard as the pennies you bent between your fingers. I don't want to be a bent penny; I want to be like clay in the hand of the divine Potter.

There's still a lot of me that remains hard and requires the Lord's strong hand. The most difficult area of my life has been forgiving my parents.

Like you, I read a lot of spiritual books. When I studied *Concentric Circles,* by Oscar Thompson, I read his emphatic statement that forgiveness is a necessary part of our missionary journey. Unless we can forgive, we cannot move on. I vividly remember throwing the book across the room after reading those convicting words. I was ready to tell the world about Jesus, but I did not want to forgive my parents. I felt justified to keep them "on the hook" for all the pain and grief I have suffered because of their weaknesses.

By the grace of God, I have finally been able to let my parents off the hook. As I experienced God's forgiveness for my own hurtful ways, I had no choice but to follow His example of forgiveness. Being forgiven and forgiving others has released me and set me free from the chains of bitterness that entangled me. Now, my energy can be used in more positive ways. How I would love to tell you my life is like a fairy tale with all of us living happily ever after. I do have an inner peace and an assurance of eternal happiness. I struggled through my relationship with my parents, attempting to put the pieces of my life together like a puzzle. My parents were not able to make this journey with me. Confronting all the issues necessary to make the pieces fit was too painful for them.

My husband and I have chosen not to smoke, drink or serve alcohol in our home. Because of this decision, my parents refused to visit. I accepted that as an indication of the disease of alcoholism, yet I still fight those feelings of rejection. There was a nagging temptation to make everything seem okay by pretending that it was . . . but in reality, it was not. In addition to alcoholism, Daddy suffers from throat cancer, and my mother has a mass in her lung. Her refusal to have a biopsy or any form of treatment is frustrating. It is hard to watch them both continue to inhale the smoke that is destroying their bodies.

At this time, our communication is strained and limited. Daddy rarely speaks, and Mother has the tendency to resort to our past patterns. Her words seem biting and destructive; mine become fearful and defensive.

The most positive conversations occur between my parents and my children. I encourage the phone calls, and I grieve that I am unable to share that kind of communication. How I wish I had with them the kind of relationship I had with you and Nana.

Pop Pop, I don't believe it was God's perfect will for my family to turn out this way. I thank Him that He has filled in so many of the empty spaces with many people in my life. I know I will see my parents in heaven, for both of them have accepted Jesus Christ as their personal Savior. In heaven, they will have perfect bodies. My father will feel no need for alcohol. My mother can rest in the arms of our heavenly Father, finally able to see that He is the One in control.

After thirty-six years, Aunt Clare helped me to get in contact with my brother, Dickie. Although his path was strewn with obstacles, it has become smoother during the last several years. God has blessed him with a wife who loves him in the way he deserves to be loved. I believe Pauline was sent by God to meet his needs. The future looks hopeful for Dickie and me. He remembers you as I do, Pop Pop—with love.

A few years ago, a friend shared one of her most cherished books with me. It was called *The Robins Are Back,* by Henry Roberts. As I read the book, I felt it had been written just for me. It offers a message of hope. Henry explains that we all experience winters in our lives, times when everything appears dead and cold. However, no matter how bad the winter may be, the seasons change, spring returns, and the robins come back.

I look back on my life, and I can see so many winters...yet so many springs to follow.

Sometimes it seemed as if I had to wait a long time for the robins to return. I believe now that each time, God was making me stronger.

> Those who wait on the Lord
> Shall renew their strength;
> They shall mount up
> with wings like eagles.
>
> —Isaiah 40:31, NKJV

Thank you for your strong, praying hands that guided me in the direction of the eagles and pointed the way to Jesus, Pop Pop. How I long for my spirit to soar and enjoy the same kind of intimacy you shared with our Father! My spirit was too crushed to see He was there all along, hiding me "in the shadow of [His] wings" (Ps. 17:8).

Over a period of two years, I have written letters of gratitude and confession to significant people in my life. Writing these letters has renewed my strength. I see clearly that God has been faithful.

Through the tender care of many people, Jesus was healing my wounded spirit.

After the healing, I found I was still weighed down by my own lack of forgiveness. Reliving the events recorded in my letters has been a heavenly process. As I yielded my will into God's hands, He was able to take my unforgiveness, press out the bitterness and mold a set of wings on my heart. Once again, He's brought the robins back...and this time, I'm ready to fly.

Thank you for showing me how.

XIX

Readers

Dear Readers,

Thank you for sharing my journey.

When I wrote the preceding letter to my dear grandfather, I had planned it to be the last letter of my book. I had even decided the name of the book would be *Ready to Fly.* I could not foresee at the time that the Lord was writing His own ending for my book, an ending that exceedingly and abundantly surpassed my limited expectations.

It embarrasses me now to think the writings of my journey could end with the image of myself as a bird flying off into the sky like Superman. However, I do believe that as the Lord was remolding my heart, He also filled it with His Spirit. Because of that Spirit, I did feel as if I had soared above and beyond the pain of my past. Without that winged Spirit, I never would have been equipped to handle what I was about to face. The little bird I fancied myself to be was about to fly into a storm.

I experienced the proverbial "calm before the storm," as my mother was blessed with a one-year, spontaneous remission of the cancer in her lung. Writing my book had allowed me to expel much of the hurt and pain I had held against her for years. Our relationship, though far from ideal, had healthy boundaries that protected both of us. My relationship with my father remained distant. However, I did not fill the space between us with bitterness and condemnation as I once had. Without those two things pulling me down, I did feel as if I were flying.

During this time, Lindsey began high school, and

Bobby began middle school. At times, I felt as if I were flying around in circles as they tried their adolescent wings. Adjusting to their independence was a challenge, but I whispered prayers of thanksgiving that our battles were fought over the dirty socks and candy wrappers on their bedroom floors and not more serious issues.

While I was whispering grateful prayers for my children, I was shouting hallelujahs for my husband. In fall 1997, he attended the Promise Keepers Rally in Washington, D.C. He apologized because he was going to be gone for my birthday, but I can't think of a better birthday present than the gift I received in his spirit of renewal. My heart is warmed as I remember the way Rob looked when he returned. There is nothing more beautiful to behold than the face of one who has been with the Lord. Rob has truly been a "promise keeper." I have watched him grow in all his demanding roles with a humble, yet quietly bold, manner. I thank God that my children have such a strong role model.

I continued to glide through my grace-filled days, tempted to feel almost spiritually smug that the Lord had personally taught me to fly. But the sunny skies began to grow darker when my mother called to report that her last X-ray had revealed the mass in her lung had almost doubled in size. That was September 1997. She died on February 6, 1998.

I have been remembering what it was like. In some ways, it seems more real now than it did then. At the time, it was like walking through a bad dream. Lately, I have been realizing how horrible it is to watch cancer literally eat someone away from the inside out.

After I learned the tumor was growing, I called my mother every day. At first, we talked as if nothing had happened. She continued her daily lifestyle as long as she could.

Veterans Day was her last day to go out with her friends. She no longer could fight the war going on in her body. I remember the date because my dad marked it as the day he stopped going to his local pub. He made up his mind to stay in the trenches with my mother. I am proud of the way he took care of her. Watching her suffer brought him to repentance. Almost every day, he thanked her for their years together, and he asked her to forgive him for all the times he had hurt her in the past. She responded tenderly and graciously.

The week before Thanksgiving, her voice got weaker over the phone. I was not sure she would live until we could get there. She was so weak the night we arrived that Bobby was afraid to go to sleep because he thought she would be dead in the morning.

By the grace of God, she recovered some strength the next day, Thanksgiving Day, and I will always be thankful. She was able to eat with us at the table. Her weight loss was not significant, and, other than being a little weaker and not being able to see well, she was still the same old "Grammy" to her grandchildren. That was the last time Lindsey and Bobby saw my mother. I am grateful they did not have to see her the way I saw her during the following months.

After we left, it was discovered she had pneumonia. Her doctor prescribed an antibiotic and told her it was time to call in Hospice. The antibiotic cleared up the pneumonia, and she regained some of her spunk.

When my Aunt Anita, my mother's youngest sister, went to stay with her, I made plans to be there at the same time. We both knew God had a greater plan when we realized we had scheduled the same flight out of Atlanta. The trip we shared to Melbourne was an anointed time, a gift from God.

My mother was as kind and appreciative as I have

ever seen her. She was also funny. I began to recognize little things about her that are just like me. Certain ways she moved her hands or cracked a joke were uncanny reflections of myself. For the first time in my life, I felt pleased that she and I had similarities.

As the days slipped by, my mother was unable to walk to the bathroom alone. My father welcomed our visit so he could have a chance to sleep through the night. The night before I was to go home was my turn to be "on night call." I remember that night tenderly. At one point, she looked at me and asked me if I had forgiven her for all the things she had done. I told her I had and asked her to forgive me for the bitterness I had harbored for the past several years. That night was a significant part in God's plan for both of our lives.

As the bitterness toward my mother was erased, bitterness toward my father began to return and escalate. Knowing my mother was in good hands with my aunt and me gave him an excuse to go to the bar. He also felt the need to do less and eagerly allowed us to do more. I watched familiar patterns resurface. When I left their house to return home, I felt I had made peace with my mother and was willing to close the door forever on my father. Thinking I might never see my mother alive again, I planned to come back for the funeral and then leave my father alone. I figured he would be content to spend his remaining days in a bar.

God had other plans. He had worked too hard on my heart to allow it to harden again. My aunt stayed a week after I left. Once she was gone, my mother rapidly went down. She became more demanding and less cooperative. Hearing the desperation in my father's voice, I returned to help.

My mother began to get agitated. She was ready to die but impatient with the dying process. She experienced an opposite reaction to the sedatives she was taking. The tender, sweet woman my Aunt Anita and I had lovingly nursed became the vicious, treacherous woman I had feared in my childhood. She lashed out with cruel remarks and unrelenting demands to my father and me literally day and night. Because she was dying, both of us felt too guilty not to try to please her. But no matter how hard we tried, she was never satisfied. My father became so nervous I told him to go to the bar. I could hardly believe the words were coming from my mouth, but I just couldn't deal with both of them.

When he returned, glazed over and numbed from the alcohol, I felt I had stepped back into a rerun of my childhood. I prayed to God for the strength to endure. I wanted to do the right thing. I wanted to obey the fourth commandment, "Honor your father and your mother," but deep down, I wished I were someone else's daughter. God knew my heart, for I am His daughter. It was still part of His plan to bring beauty from ashes. The next day, after trying to calm one of my mother's vehement tirades, my father came into the den to talk to me. He commented he had never seen her act like that. I looked him straight in the eyes and said, "Daddy, that is the woman I grew up with. That green medicine she took made her act exactly like this. Only I was a scared little girl, and when my whiney, mousy ways enraged her, she beat me. Don't you remember the bruises, Daddy? Did you really believe I fell down the steps that many times? You didn't care. You didn't know. You were a selfish man who cherished your time in a bar more than your time with your wife and child. She couldn't cope, so she took the green medicine, and it made her act like this. Imagine dealing with this as a child. I couldn't tell you because I was ashamed. I thought I was a very bad little girl. I didn't want you to know Mommy beat me like that because I thought it was my fault. Now do you understand why I have pulled away these last several years?"

Writing it is almost as hard as saying it was. Even with all the healing and recovery, it still hurts. I cried and cried after I finished this speech. I am writing through tears now.

When I looked up, I saw my father was crying, too. He said he knew I was right; he was able to put a lot of missing pieces together. He admitted he was selfish, and he was sorry. And this is when the beauty came from the ashes, my dear reader. I forgave him. Forgiveness does not change the past, but it does enlarge the future. My dad and I began a new relationship that day.

We began working as a team instead of two strangers trying to survive.

Knowing I would have to return home soon, I persuaded my father to hire a nurse to take the night shift. When I left, I knew it was probably the last time I would see my mother alive. I also knew I would continue to see my father with new eyes.

On the plane ride home, I thanked God for allowing me to see, with adult eyes, the devastating impact drugs had on my mother. No longer did I feel she was a mean mommy and I was a bad little girl. Her body was just having an adverse reaction to a sedative. I was a victim of that reaction as a child, but the events of the previous week helped me to see I was now the victor. I know by whose strength I was able to overcome.

My mother continued to get worse after I left. We think maybe the cancer went to her brain.

My heart aches as I remember how my mother spent her remaining days on earth. More than anything, she wanted to die in her own bed, but because she became uncontrollable, my father was forced to hospitalize her. She fought every attempt by the hospital staff to keep her in bed.

The doctors and nurses tried many forms of sedatives, but, as before, they seemed to work in reverse. Finally, her body could fight no more, and she slipped into a coma.

Someone had told me that the hearing was the last thing to go, so before we ended our conversation, I told my father to get near her ear and tell her anything he wanted to say to her before she died.

I went to my Bible study the next day and asked my friends to pray for a miracle. Together, we prayed that God would graciously allow my mother to give some form of recognition to my Dad before she died.

Later that day, I discovered that at just about the time we were praying, Dad leaned over Mom and whispered in her ear that he loved her. To his surprise, she opened her eyes and reached up and hugged his neck. We do indeed have a God who answers prayers. Praise Him, praise Him, praise Him!

When he called to tell me, I explained the events of the morning. He knew also that it was a gift from God.

It is hard to write this as if I were just reporting events. My heart is overflowing with grateful praise for my Jesus and my church, my true family of believers. That family knows no denomination; they just know their Father.

My father told me my mother no longer looked like herself. She was bloated and puffy. I knew then that the cancer probably had reached her liver, and the end was near.

I called the hospital that night and asked the nurse to put the phone to my mother's ear. I read the Twenty-third Psalm and prayed the Lord's Prayer. I could hear her grunt and moan softly. My last words to her were "It's okay, I know what you are trying to say. I know you love me, and I love you, too. In a little while, you'll be with Jesus. One day, I'll see you again, and everything will be perfect and beautiful. I love you, Mommy. Thank you for my life."

Five hours later, my dad called and said, "She's gone." He didn't want me to come right away. He wanted some time alone. Because she wished to be cremated, the funeral had to be put off a little longer than usual. A childhood friend of my father came to stay with him. Rob and I came a few days later. The funeral was on Valentine's Day, 1999.

If you remember, in my letter to Bobby, it was on Valentine's Day when God allowed my heart to begin to crack. Little by little, the pain of my infected past oozed out. But look what God has done! He has given me a new heart!

My dad's last days were so hard for both of us. He had received a bad report on a CT scan May 3, and he died June 4, 2000. Those days in between were the most challenging of my life. As I watched cancer snatch away his body and mind, my heart ached for him—such a big strong man reduced to helplessness.

When I arrived at his hospital room, I found an empty bed on one side of him and a naked, skinny man grunting gibberish on the other side. I feared the empty bed meant I had arrived too late. I ran to the nurses' station and frantically blurted out, "Where is Mr. Siegman?" Calmly, a nurse led me back to the room. "There he is," she said. I didn't recognize him. There were only brief interludes when he recognized me.

During the following days, I kept a watch by his bed, feeding him water from a sponge stick. It reminded me of the many little sparrows Lindsey found fallen from their nests. Each time she found one, she believed she could nurse it back to life. Sadly, every one of Lindsey's birds died. And Daddy died. Years of alcohol and tobacco killed his lungs and liver. However, I know deep in my heart that although his eyes were deceived, God's eyes were on the sparrow, and He was watching over Daddy. A dear friend and mentor of mine, Mary Martin, counseled and comforted me over the phone during that hard time. I believe it was a word of prophecy when she told me the song "His Eye Is On the Sparrow" was God's word for me.

So many dirty secrets were exposed as I cleaned out his house during that last week. Although he tried to take a new road after mother died, he soon turned back. I was so proud when he volunteered in the soup kitchen. It saddened me when he slipped in the shower, hurting his back, and was unable to stand and ladle the soup. It was then that he began again to spend all his free time and money in bars. Every sermon I have heard about being able to know everything about someone by examining his checkbook is true. The devil had reordered his priorities.

My father's last days brought forth a myriad of painful emotions. It is only by the strength of my Savior that I was able to endure the dark days at his bedside and the darker nights at his house. At times I felt alone. Rob was only able to stay the first two days before returning to work. Once again, God sent His angels: Lisa, Daddy's caseworker; Rev. Robert Bruckart, the hospital chaplain; and Daddy's friends Earl and Cindy provided a lifeline for me. God even provided an oasis in the desert when two tenderhearted ladies, Jane and Beanie, found me crying in the hospital chapel and invited me to go to a Wednesday night church service. I had a new appreciation of what it meant to be a member of the family of

God. I will be forever grateful to the pastor and members of the Oceanside Evangelical Free Church. They truly ministered to me during a time of great need. I can't imagine surviving without them.

There came a point when we had to transfer Daddy to a nursing home. I felt somewhat comforted that I was able to place him in the same facility he had chosen for my mother. Before they moved him, I went to his new room and decorated the small bulletin board with pictures. I wanted the people who saw him to know how he once looked. That frail, bony man was not the handsome Duke Siegman I knew. It made me sad to think that no one knew that but me. However, I did learn to appreciate those who care for dying patients. Each time I came to see him, his hair was combed and he was clean. Although he was unresponsive, he was treated tenderly and with dignity. I was humbled and impressed by the staff at Tandem Health Care in Melbourne, Florida.

I hung a large American flag in Daddy's room. I was hoping he would at least recognize the colors. He was always so proud to be a World War II veteran. I was really hoping he would die on Memorial Day. He never wanted a funeral or church service, and I thought Memorial Day would honor his memory. God had other plans. He knew exactly what day He had planned for Daddy's homecoming. A greater work was being done in him and in me as we suffered through his dying days. I believe both of us were dying to ourselves.

As his heavy, labored breathing became shallow and faint, so also faded my resentment. As I let him go into the arms of Jesus, I let go of those last entangling strings of the past. When he left this world, I was left with the peace that passes understanding.

He died early on a Sunday morning. I had an overwhelming desire to go to a church service. I wanted to worship and praise my Jesus for His faithfulness through those final days. I found a small church near the hospital. It was called His Place. I had no idea it was a church with recovery ministry for alcoholism and drug abuse. During the service, a young man came forward to confess Jesus as his Savior. After the service, he was going to leave immediately for a rehab center. Echoes of praise were voiced from the congregation. A member of the church staff who had met me before the service introduced me. She announced that my dad had died. She asked that the service that day be his memorial service. He said he never wanted a church service, but I believe God arranged this one just for me. I know he was blessed all the way from heaven when they dedicated the trumpet solo to him. The song was "Victory in Jesus." When the congregation joined in to sing the refrain, I felt the angels in heaven must have been singing along. It was a victorious day. Daddy joined his Savior forever.

Thank you for allowing me to share my heart with you. Thank you for allowing me to tell you about myself and those people God has used in my life. The greatest joy is that He is not finished with me yet. He is still writing the pages of my life.

> He has showed me, my Reader,
> what is good.
> And what does the Lord require of me?
> To act justly and to love mercy
> and to walk humbly with my God.
>
> —MICAH 6:8, NIV, PERSONALIZED

I had wanted to call my book *Ready to Fly.* I think now I will call it *Ready to Walk.*

—MICHELLE
JANUARY 25, 1999

XX

EPILOGUE

MOTHER AND DADDY

Dear Mother and Daddy,

As I write this letter, the tiny lights on the Christmas tree sparkle and greet me from across the room. This has been the best Christmas of my life. Lindsey is home from Ringling College for Christmas break. We are so proud of her; she has matured into a lovely, talented young woman. She received her first semester grades a few days ago. They were great! She will maintain her academic honor scholarship. This is quite an accomplishment in her field, because she is evaluated on her art as well as academics. I think she inherited your creativity, Mommy. Hopefully, she will become the animator she's always wanted to be. The dragons that once haunted her have been captured and brought to life at the end of her pencils. She has found a way to express herself to the world. In many ways, that is exactly what I have done in writing this book.

I praise Jesus that I have the assurance that both of you are now in heaven. It gives me peace to think of you now fully restored with perfect bodies and minds.

Christmas must be beautiful in heaven. My sweet little Mommy, I imagine you decorating the skies with evergreen garlands as bright as emeralds. How you loved to decorate. I have decorated my house this year as never before. I thought of you with a smile and a tear as I added a Christmas touch to every corner. I am forty-seven years old now. For at least the last twenty years, people have been giving me little mice figurines for Christmas. Everywhere I look, a small whiskered face peeks out with a bit of Christmas cheer. Rob says it looks like the house is infested. When I was growing up, I used to pretend I was like Cinderella with little mice friends taking care of me. I don't have to pretend anymore. I see now that God really does send His angels to watch over us. There is joy in every corner of my life, Mommy. I feel so free this Christmas. I know that you and Daddy are also free at last.

Daddy, you have found healing now under the wings of your Savior. You are in a place where there is no more deception. Addictions are not allowed to fill empty holes because there are no empty holes in heaven. There is only fullness of joy in the presence of God. How peaceful I feel knowing that you are in the presence and glory of God. Every unclean thing is washed away.

The day before you died proved to be a significant point in my life, Daddy. Originally, I had decided I would not return to your house. Yet there was something telling me everything was not quite right. I started wondering if I had locked the door. I tried to dismiss the nagging thought of having to return to check as just another trick from the devil. The still, small voice was persistent. I finally went back. Sure enough, the door was unlocked. As I pulled out the keys and locked the door, a sense of peace swept over me like a warm tide. I returned to the hospital to spend your last day with you.

The words of the Scripture at the church service I attended following your death brought that experience into the light:

> "I will place on his shoulder the key to the house of David; what he opens no one can shut, and what he shuts no one can open. I will drive him like a peg into a firm place; he will be a seat of honor for the house of his father. All the glory of his family will hang on him: its offspring and offshoots—all its lesser vessels, from the bowls to the jars."
>
> —ISAIAH 22:22–23

The Lord gave me the key, Mom and Dad. He taught me through the writing of this book to lock the door on the past. Just as I had to clean out your house, lock the door and walk away, I had to allow Jesus to clean out my heart and my mind, accept His power to lock the door and walk away with Him. I am not doomed to repeat the destructive patterns of the past. I pray my life will honor both of you. I have a godly husband and a healthy marriage. My precious children are a new generation. May they bring glory to their Heavenly Father. I had to laugh about the last verse of Scripture referring to the bowls and the jars. I brought home the big light blue bowl you used to mix sugar cookie dough, Mommy. The door is locked to the terrible abuse of our kitchen. The bowl and jars are now filled with good memories, such as Christmas cookies. It is a time of new birth.

Christmas songs have come alive for me this year. Your handsome grandson, Bobby, has become the singer I always wanted to be. In this year's chorus production, he had a solo called "Rise Up, Shepherd." You would have been proud to see him sing. One of the African-American mothers working backstage with me asked me where he got so much soul. He sings from his heart. Praise God, his heart belongs to Jesus. One of the words repeated over and over in his solo was "Follow." I am moving on, Mom and Dad. I'm following Jesus, one step at a time—sometimes baby steps, sometimes leaps of faith. I believe I was led by the Holy Spirit to write this book. I pray it will help others to lock the doors to the past and to move on with God—to "walk in the light, as he is in the light..." (1 John 1:7).

Thank you for giving me my life, Mom and Dad. May it give glory to our Lord. Amen.

—MICHELLE

DECEMBER 29, 2000